Missing Persons

Edited by
Deborah Coy
Guest Editor Barbora Cowles

Cover art by Larry Schulte

BEATLICK PRESS
Albuquerque, NM

Missing Persons ©2019 Deborah Coy
the title from the poem by Scott Wiggerman

ISBN 9781729706954

Publisher: Beatlick Press
Albuquerque, NM

Printed in the United States

Cover art "Yellow Buttons" by Larry Schulte

Dedication

To all who struggle with this condition and to their families, friends, and their caretakers. Know you are not alone.

Editor's Introductions
Deborah Coy

When the tragedy of dementia strikes a family the world changes for them. As our population ages this situation becomes more and more common.

I dealt with dementia in my grandmother, my grandfather, my father, my beloved mother-in-law, and now a close friend. Each instance presented itself differently. Sometimes it came on slowly and lasted for years. In my father's case it came on instantly and completely and lasted only a few weeks. No matter how it manifests itself in individuals it takes a terrible toll on those around them.

My decision to tackle this subject was a long in coming. The tipping point was when our friend (Barbora's husband Joe) was afflicted. It had struck our generation and I could no longer let it go anymore. I decided to shoot for the book I would have liked to read while caretaking my mother-in-law and in seeing others I love affected.

I feel it is important for people to know that they are not alone. I have been joined with other authors who explore the multiple manifestations of the disease. You will find stories of anger and love. Even humor finds a place in this anthology.

While we all hope for cures, we also desperately need support and resources to cope. Barbora Cowles has included a resource sheet of organizations that are helping her.

The process of arranging this presented a big challenge so, with a few exceptions, I randomly placed the contributions hoping that no work would be ignored.

I hope all who read this are comforted.

Barbora Cowles

Our journey began on 14 December 2016. My husband went to bed one person and woke up another with a chunk of his memory gone.

It took another six months before he was diagnosed with beginning Alzheimer's Disease. Friends ask me if he has dementia.

Dementia is a term that includes all types of cognitive impairment. So I tell them yes, he has Alzheimer's which is a form of dementia.

Alzheimer's does not usually come on so quickly like his. But then, there is nothing usual about Alzheimer's. My husband has been more or less on a plateau ever since that morning. His progression has been slow. Some days he is more confused than others. But, that is true for all of us. We all have good days and bad days.

Since that time, I have taken a caregiver's class at the local Alzheimer's Association. I've taken a number of other classes as well. They have helped me to understand what is happening with him and how I can best help him. The classes have also helped me to understand what is happening with me and how to take care of myself.

I am so lucky I have a person who does respite for me once a week for a couple of hours. I can get away knowing my husband is spending time with someone I trust, who is kind and funny and supportive. We have a small group of friends who visit or whom we visit. It is important to stay social. Isolating is not good for a caregiver or the loved one.

I attend a support group twice a month. The group's members range from beginners like me to people who have been caregivers for years to those who have survived their loved ones. There is always a box of Kleenex on the table and there is laughter as well. We share information on where to go, what to do next and "what worked for me in your situation". There is often no fix, but at least we can talk about what is happening and the other people in the group understand. Just being able to share with no judgement coming at us is worthwhile.

If you are caregiving someone, I recommend you find classes and a group. You might have to try out several groups, but don't give up. You can't do this alone. There is help, sometimes we need to seek it out.

Useful links

These links are specific to New Mexico. There are most likely similar sites in your area.

https://www.alz.org/newmexico

https://rememberychronicles.blogspot.com/

https://makedementiayourbitch.com/

https://www.alzheimersreadingroom.com/

http://teepasnow.com/
Teepa has some great videos on YouTube.

http://www.nmaging.state.nm.us/silver-alert.aspx
An excellent service for those who wander on foot or in a vehicle.

http://www.nmaging.state.nm.us/aaa.aspx

Your state will have an agency on aging and senior services with good information.

For those outside of New Mexico you may also contact Alzheimer's Disease International. https://www.alz.co.uk

Table of Contents

Note to Self

Be thankful for the dishes waiting to be washed.
Be thankful you are not alone in your car
unwrapping a meal under parking lot lights.
Be thankful you can feel the pain
that stabs your back when you rise
to meet the day. Be thankful
when you put on your own pants, one leg at a time
because nothing lasts forever. The day is coming
when you will no longer be able
to tie your own shoes. You will know something
is wrong but you will not be able recognize your own
hunger. Be thankful she is there to feed you,
forgive you and remember your name
after you have forgotten hers.

Missing Persons

That girl whose father
walked away from his family,
not to be heard from again:

I never thought of
my 95-year-old grandmother
as that girl,

but here she is,
conversing with him daily
until he turns

and walks off—again.
Through tears she asks,
Why would he do this?

I wasn't done talking!
She's confused
by his smooth skin,

his full head of hair—
It's like he doesn't age—
never mind that

eight decades have passed
since he became a ghost.
Last night he was supposed

to meet her at the drug store;
another day, the park.
Locations change,

but one thing is constant:
the turning away.
Rumor was he went west,

and now that she's
in a home in Arizona,
she thinks she might find him.

She may be closer
than any of us
can see.

Is it Dementia, or Just ADD?

We grey women poets
commiserate about
these days when we can't
remember, you know,
the name of that favorite
movie star, the blonde one,
who was in that really
great picture we loved.
You know, the whatsis story,
about those thingies
they made in what
was that country again?
Or, alternatively, what
we ate for dinner last night.
If it wasn't for keeping
a sense of humor,
memory would be
our least favorite topic.
We remind each other,
our favorite organ is brains,
(especially since some
others seem to have taken
flight, or a vacation
at any rate.)
Hearts irregular, uteruses
(oh, my God, my spelling is trashed,)
absent or revolting,
a gynecological mess, at best,
hands arms and feet, full of arthritis.
We pray and console that
our senses won't desert us.

4

Still, how will we
know to remember what
it was we forgot, like
those long purple fruit,
divine when fried in cracker crumbs,
(may my mind not become crackers just yet.)
Oh, eggplants, of course—
though I doubt
planting eggs would come to much.
I hope to remember
my grandchildren's names,
though they rapidly multiply
and double in size,
I love them anyway.
If I forget the important things,
I hope they'll take me, like Lenny
from *Mice and Men*
out to the woods
where the puppies play,
and shoot me.
Still, when one of us
forgets a word, we all laugh
uproariously
because the next to forget
is probably you or me.
What was that
chingadera called again?
I swear to God, I still feel sixteen.

What We Don't Talk About

In this ragged little town
on its patch of prairie where we live,
lightning storms and hope of rain
kept us entertained all week.

Ivy Harris' dogs barked all night and her
neighbor, Jim Haines, complained about it
at the Hilltop Café over his coffee and eggs,
spooning runny whites to his whiskered mouth.

Buster Harmon sits in a booth alone chewing
bacon and sopping cream gravy with his biscuit.
No one here ever says 'simple minded' or 'crazy."
just cause he lived with his mother for 58 years.

And now she is gone. Her heart gave out
after raising nine children on a sandy land
cotton farm, burying two husbands
and looking after Buster all those years.

He could be thinking of his future, his only
life utterly changed at her passing. Or, maybe
he's wondering what he will do now that his
family is selling the farmhouse where he sat

in the same chair to eat, day in and day out,
all of his life. But he says nothing of this, not a word.
No one else mentions it either. Out here,
we don't broadcast ever damned thing we know.

Thelma Giomi

Quantum Barrier

My mind is fine.
Just fine.
It's the doors.
Psychologists studied them.
Every doorway,
Every passage through
Triggers an event boundary.
So, when my mind goes blank,
And I can't even grab the edge of
Why I came into this room,
It's the doors.
It's the doors
That separate thoughts,
Neatly filing them in one room,
Creating a blank slate in the next.
So, it's not Alzheimer's or an aging brain,
Or even preoccupation with a thousand daily chores
That accounts for my memory lapses,
It's none of these.
It's just the damn doors.

Rich Boucher

Whenever I Get An Idea,
A Light Bulb Full of Gunpowder
Appears Above My Head

through the window
at this moment
an unsettling sight:

all over this neighborhood
(made from genuine and authentic
tan suburban afternoon)
houses are dismantling themselves
in slow motion

you can see it

debris rising up into the sky
everywhere you look

beds, dressers, walls, sconces,
sinks still full of water, roofs, chairs,
everything *and all else that isn't everything*
floating up into an overcast
the color of an unplugged light bulb

so when the salesman pounds on my door
and rings the bell at the same time,
what am I supposed to do?

supplicate? listen carefully to his pitch?
appreciate his enthusiasm?
why doesn't he notice
what I can see plain as day out there?

8

aren't there more pressing matters
needing our attention?

if, from here on out, it becomes necessary
to live in that inclement, vibrating and emotional hospital
where the people who can't think right anymore
wind up spending the rest of their lives,
I want it to be my decision.

The Meaning of That Lilac Bush

In your desperate search for reason,
you scan the world like a lunatic:
What is the meaning of that lilac
bush, that backyard fence, this fountain pen?
You speculate that every object
has a purpose beyond what you can see
as you wander past the Christmas tree,
the coffee machine, the writing desk.
Where did you go when you went away?
Some say you had a stroke, others think
amnesia, perhaps a psychic break.
You have no memory of that day.
All you know is you love coffee,
there's snow on the ground, and you are free.

John Hicks

Not Stars. Not Us.

The stars have flicked on again,
resisting darkness, this silence.

Gravel crunches
underfoot the path among the trees,
their leaves shading memory.

You say I used to stand
in the street, and looking up,
knew where I was,
knew our stars, their names,
and a little joke about Orion.

You were angry this morning.

Light once defined darkness for me,
but now when I reach, things gray.
I feel us flickering.

There are leaves beneath my feet.
Take my hand.

Ultimate State

The great floppy sadness
descends once again out
of no where, without cause,
no forewarning. Is it my
diet, my DNA, brain chemicals?
It latches like an insect with
suction cup feet. I allow it to
feed, sit paralyzed.
Insects crawling up my arms.
I don't know what these marks
on paper are for or what they
mean. The names of things
and people are impossible
to bring to the surface. I saw
at the foot of my bed last night
a figure in a Prussian infantry
uniform. Great hat. Good colors.
He didn't answer my questions.
What's that sound? Like sand
running in my ears.
My senses are all out of whack.
I can't think straight. The neurons
are strangling each other. My
balance is precarious. I'm writing
this and wondering what it's for.
I don't want to eat. Food tastes
like Styrofoam. I walk down the
street in my bed clothes, which
is nothing at all. Strange people
escort me back to this place.
The rest of my life will be like
this only worse.

Wichita Lineman

Was Glen Campbell
changed
when he sang and played guitar
on Wichita Lineman
yet couldn't dress himself?

What is to be afraid of
if I speak nonsense
as a poet
but still
have rhythm of speech?

I will notice myself in a mirror
and try to climb out
my distractions will breed
until I can't take the strain
but I won't notice, I can hear you through the whine

I will play the piano uninhibited
my written words will play with scarves
strewn on the bed, unmade
I will not know how or why
to make a proper folded corner

Others will think I have died
I am not myself, I have changed
I will be an object
to be talked about and tested
and I'll need you more than want you

to fear that it may be coming
I do not know
I only know observations of trees
how a cat feels when it hunts
uninhibited by what others think

wonder where to find myself
aren't we all still looking?
I pause
perception
a different kind of attention

the hardest part would be
not writing
but I wouldn't know who is President
ol' Ronnie wouldn't remember either
who calls him on the hot line

I will play records backwards
and understand that secret message
from the Beatles
I will watch old movies with Charlton Heston
damn us all, we are a Planet of Apes

I will wear a trench coat
like Peter Falk in Columbo
seek to find out one more thing at the last minute
one last question, please don't forget
his wisdom and humor, his compassion

I don't want to be embarrassed
Gene Wilder's wife
almost died herself
caretaking to keep the Willy Wonka legend
from scaring the children

I will sing anyway
my brain may shrink
and forget to let my body walk
it is too complicated
it has been forgotten

I will sit next to the woman
who is very thin, with crazy hair
I will bring her coffee
she is content, she says she has everything done
the list is done, everything has a place

What satisfaction!
At last, that she knows
and only she knows where she is going
the rest of us are waiting
that Wichita Lineman listening in on the line

Lauren Camp

Five Days of a Day and a Night

Deep in July we're beside the Atlantic
where we hover
at beach streets until the sunset
excludes only one color. Such rapture

to stroll with my Dad toward the hotel
to sponge off his sweaty back. Nothing frantic
or closing. This reminds me never

to be disappointed. Are his thoughts
floating? We ramble past the corner bar
and a drag queen in yellow sequins, people's palms

chancing out dollars from a banister, the clutch
and puzzle of perspective, but he isn't pulled
to what's offered—not sparkle,

nor the evolving release
of particulars. Around us, bodies
etch to their suits in the swaggering crowds, and further

behind is the shuffling ocean, spilling out
its great polished protest.
The revelers keep close
around us in their compositions of folds

and long legs and cruising
motion. The heat makes them eager
and feasting. Dad is not where he is

but in the durable heart
of the sky or his snug mental crevices, and the waves
come forth and the waves never die.

16

Juleigh Howard-Hobson

Knowing It's Disappearing is the Worst Part

Somehow, knowing that Alzheimer's is coming mocks all one's aspirations - to tell stories, to think through certain issues ... to be recognized for one's accomplishments and hard work - in a way that old familiar death does not.—Jane Smiley

Don't tell me there's light beyond the horizon.
There's none. And I don't really give a damn
If you agree. I don't need your wise and
Loving talks about age, ad nauseaum,
Either. What I need is it all back, all
Of it, the memories I can't find, each
Shred of my inner me that somehow sprawls
And crashes at my feet...You'd think I'd reached
The point where my mind decayed enough to
Leave me in peace with my dementia... but
I haven't arrived there. Not yet. So, you
Spare me, you. You spare me the kind hand pat,
The fake smile, the happy pretense—I know
Where I'm headed and I don't want to go.

Sixty

The mind slips. Skips like a needle on an old LP
jumps randomly to another cut. The thought you were having
fast forwards into another the way the melody you were listening to
is lost in a mix with a new.
You can almost distinguish pieces of each
     but neither really
           before a third begins.

Where was I? What was I saying?
What were you?

II
Words escape.
And names from long ago are there but
yesterday's or this afternoon's depart in minutes.
(Sometimes as someone you've just met is talking
you wonder if he knows you've lost his name already.
You wonder how to get it back, how to lead him into saying it again.)

You administer small self-tests:
Where was I on Friday? Who else was there?
And Tuesday afternoon? Am I confusing it with Wednesday?
Who knows? Who cares?

Talk turns to trips taken long ago and you wonder:
Was I there? People say you were—you probably were—
but if they're wrong, you wouldn't know.

Where was I? What was I saying?
Does it matter?

III
You could retreat into how things used to be; you could take up residence
in memory—accurate or not, however that might be.
But why?
It's *now* that counts.
Here's where you are.

And it's the young who interest you,
those who are here around you—
everything stretching out before them.

They're like fawns in a long meadow at dusk
while you're one of the old trees in the shadows that border
that space where the young make plans.

You would shelter them if you could
but old trees are vulnerable to stiff winds and heavy rains.
They lose their grip in the deep slipping plates beneath the earth's surface.
They fall as if in slow motion and lie across the meadow's edge,
their tangle of roots surprisingly not so substantial as you'd guess.

The young may remember their cool shadows, the expanse of their shade.
Or they may not.

The mind slips. What was I saying? What were you?

Richard Vargas

i dream about remembering to forget

i am forgetting things. memories fade like old Polaroids left
in the sun. i tell a woman serving me breakfast that she
looks very pretty, and i introduce myself. she tells me she's
my wife and begins to cry. i don't know what to say. i don't
know. sentences are started but not finished as thoughts
drift off like red blossoms floating down the Ganges river.
i watch tv with my dog, Jack, at my side. he licks my hand
over and over. i pat his big German Rottweiler head,
say goodbye. he says he'll never leave me, no matter what
happens. my last lucid thoughts: trying to remember who
i wrote a note to, asking them to put me to sleep once and
for all when i become the equivalent of an eggplant. i hope
they don't lose that note. then i am sitting in a room with a
chair and a table. a shaft of sunlight comes through a
window and flecks of dust hang in the air as if time has
come to a standstill.

what is the dream and
what is real? am i dying
awake in my sleep?

Reptilian Brains

Crying and coughing, war comes to us.
Sheep and chickens on the stairs.
Bob Dylan is armed and dangerous.
Courts of Homeland Security with
access to yellow cake only with
passwords. Old school pandemics
jump the Pacific for Asia.
Lullabies for the miscarried.
Spinach in my teeth.
Earnest haystacks with solar
panels. Streets in ruin. People's
lives at risk. Her water broke.
The Keeper of Transit Papers
jump starts his car. A checkpoint
for suspicious activity and proper
care. Jesus Christ ends up in the
Pieta.
Fascists uprising. Ketamine as
requested. I faint like a freak.
All practice environmental
racism. Enhanced interrogation
techniques behind metal-platted
doors. It's a girl! Gentle faintest
Jonathon Living Sea Gulls. A pest
of a chance lightening up.

For a Moment

"For a minute it seemed the Bureau of Joy was calling
about a windfall blowing my way
to guarantee an eight or nine on the joy chart."
By Carl Dennis from his book *Practical Gods*;
'Gelati' is the title of the poem.

For a moment it seemed the Credenza of Laughter
was calling about a crescendo tilting
toward evening after the elders
went to bed.

For a moment it seemed the Bookcase of Departure
was calling about a page I'd missed
on the third shelf
in an honorable mystery.

For a moment it seemed the Dresser of Contemplation
was calling about a satin negligee worn
while singing the second verse
of "Row, Row, Row Your Boat."

Aeolian

He asked me if I held him responsible
for my mother's slow descent into nothingness

all those years ago. He gripped the deck railing
memory had misplaced its herding instincts but

the summer heat filled his bones with light. His rice
paper skin, his white hair game show host perfect.

Telephone wires above us murmured like harp strings.
To my father, the blue sky out here was the sweltering Pacific,

war seen from underneath the ocean, a still breathing thing, Leyte Bay.
I asked myself, at this age, the currents of rivers so much

swifter than before, clots of shore ice breaking off &
floating rapidly towards some endless summer, was truth more

important than beauty? I answered him:
                                                    Of course not.

All recriminations silenced is the beauty of spring's first scented
rain, a loved one's inevitable absence leaving every darkened door ajar.

A poem heard only when recited by the wind.

Marathon

Today the Duke City Marathon
was run, along Albuquerque's
Bosque Trail.

I was not among the runners
from seniors to teens; instead

I carefully rode the trail on
my beloved mountain bike

parallel to the crowded main trail.
Yet for all my care, for the third time

in a month (and now riding the Aldo
Leopold single-track, off-road loop)

I crashed: I smashed my nose and
broke my front teeth in half.

A major symptom of Binswanger's
Encephalopathy is the loss of balance.

Others include depression, anti-
social behavior, irritability

slurred speech, memory loss and
withdrawal into isolation—silence.

Binswanger's Neurological Disease
is degenerative: there is no cure.

24

A child abandoning training wheels
I am relearning how to ride a bike.

Falling into the icy, jagged
cataract of depression

knowing I cannot climb back
no human looking down at me. trapped.

suffocating. Increasingly detached
from my abilities, my family, my

dear, darling spouse, my life
I watch the world move on.

¿Recuerdas?

He's on the patio when she arrives—
he prefers to be outside.
He grew up outdoors, rode horses first,
tractors then, mowers, balers,
plowed and harvested his father's fields.
That's all gone except for memories
that surface every now and then.
(He might hear faint freeway noise
and confuse it with equipment from the farm.)

She takes his hand when she arrives.
"Holá, cariño," she smiles. He doesn't know her.
She pulls up a chair beside him,
opening a book of photos—
their wedding, more than fifty years ago.
"¿Recuerdas, mi amor. Recuerdas?"
He doesn't. But he smiles. He doesn't talk much anymore.

She plays a song on her device
and a flame ignites behind his eyes.
He smiles as she begins to sing; he hums along—
a song they used to dance to some sixty years ago.
¿Tú recuerdas, corazón? Yo sé que sí."
She holds his hand, they sit and sing together—
he and this *extraña* who seems to know him.

Mary Ellen Kelly

Beneath Their Silent Wings

Three owls in one day is good news to me.
No sound of their flight through the hemlock treetops.
A flutter in my chest, a twig dropped, a branch disrupted
send my gaze upward in time for the landing
and one feathered head turning to see me
better than I have ever seen myself.
Oh that owls could be my mirrors!

My mother has forgotten what a mirror does
and wonders what that woman wants from her.
She stays away from the bathroom
just to be safe.
I bathe her in her room, encourage her to eat
the easy food on the spoon.
Eventually she opens her mouth like a baby bird.

Last Friday I drove to work,
my husband at the theater rehearsing
"A Little Night Music,"
our teenager asleep in her room
recovering from cramps,
and a mother in her bed of twisted blankets.
"Everyone's fine—I'm fine—They're fine"
I sang an off-key tune of my own creation,
then switched to the reliable "Give My Regards to Broadway."

In class, worry clung to my lecture
like the spiders of my mother's hallucinations.
I left early to the sound of applause for a no-homework day.

Every road bump flipped my stomach.
I turned left at the first green light,
floored it for all the yellows,
buried too many "What ifs" beneath
the gas pedal.
What if she left a burner on, walked outside,
crossed the highway?
Faster. Faster.

Home was my child making a peanut butter sandwich,
my mother in bed, eyes moving beneath closed lids,
the moon wandering in her sky blue mind,
and me with a decision.

I dialed the old phone,
reserved a room with a door
that opens onto a yellow lined carpet,
pointing the undeniable way, like an arrow,
toward the parlor of stuffed chairs.
Nobody walks away from this "vacation."
Nobody in those significantly soft chairs
will ever know the 2-4-6-8 "get-out" combination.
They will be told over and over again –
The bus is on its way.

On the morning of deliverance,
"Better" was a stumble.
It stuck in my throat.
My husband heard it. Nodded. Said the word clearly.
My mother smiled at the sound of his deep voice.
Our daughter opened her mouth,
then closed it
lips tight
eyes staring at the space
between love and lies.

On whose behalf did I say
she will be better off
among her own new kind?

On whose behalf do I admit
I need the owls?

Marmika Paskiewicz

The Nuns' Tale

For over 60 years they watched them, tested them
as they walked up and down Good Counsel Hill—
some stayed bright   some grew dim

sat in rocking chairs with blank eyes
some trimmed the cherry tree, said novenas
without halting.

Cutting through cold flesh   bone
after hearts had stopped
they saw the tangles that mean disease
wild horses in both brains
ones who had faded   ones who remained bright
both brains the same

Who says it will happen   to her to him to me
Who says?

(Note: One of the results of a study of 678 Sisters of Notre Dame in Minnesota, on autopsy, showed that brains that showed signs of Alzheimer's—tangles, bundles—did not always mean the person actually developed dementia.)

Gayle Lauradunn

Grandfather

Grandfather sits in the nursing home, his wheelchair
      strapped down so he won't rock himself to the floor
   again and hit his head gash it open, open, he

wants to see the blood. He rips the pajamas covering
      the stumps to look for his legs. At eighty-eight he
   threw his last calf for branding, his fingers losing

their quickness, their quickness with the rope and
      the calk kicked him shattering his hip. He planted
   corn and alfalfa, raised five children, two

children to their death. He slaughtered cows, pigs
      wrung, wrung necks of chickens. He asks now
   he asks whose girl are you I'm Annie B's

Grandpa Annie B's. And he asks how old am I
      how old. Ninety-seven Grandpa ninety-seven.
   Too old he says too old whose girl are you

Annie B's Grandpa Annie B's. Too old he says too
      old and rocks, rocks hard the chair tied to the floor.

Puzzle Pieces

My father fell away by bits
like pieces from a puzzle, lost.
One at a time: A piece of sky,
from the garden, one lonely leaf,
from the mountainside, a piece of slate.
Some pieces counted more than most,
some less: who was president in '68
mattered less than
change your clothes
after the body's come undone
and spilled itself for everyone
to see and laugh.
Then shame, another puzzle piece
is gone at last.

At first it seemed a minor thing,
these insignificant losses,
the design still clear, over all.
Then memory, ours, filled in the holes
when we recalled what used to be.
Later, he became abstract;
scattered color, bits of thought,
the canvas emptying itself,
more missing than we could remember,
then gone, even to himself.
Memory reminds us all,
like leaves along a forest floor
become the earth, then turn to stone.

Kelly Morgan

A Circus for the Elderly

Grandma's birthday was the first time
we all gathered at the nursing home
at the same time
and my brother made a pumpkin pie
because pumpkin was her favorite
and though she never ate anymore
in a perhaps subconscious solicitation of death
she said yes to a piece of pumpkin pie
and surprised the hell out of us all
and every now and then she would look at the pie
and ask who made it and say it looked good
and ask for a piece as if she hadn't had one yet
and we began to wonder if she was tricking us
if the whole damned dementia was a ruse
until we remembered where she was
realized that any functional memory
would not accept a place like this

Juleigh Howard-Hobson

The Queen Is Dead

From the outside the beehive hooks
You with a charmingness that brooks
No discord. Placed under a tree
Just so, near flowers carefully
Chosen. Everything by the book:
Painted, tidy, trim. Keepers took
Care that this—by hook or by crook—
Appeared so, even if only
From the outside.
Because once the box has been shook,
The lid opened, each empty nook
Held up and inspected, you'll see
Nothing. The inner colony's
Collapsed, no matter how it looks
From the outside.

Take

Take a nap, take a walk, take a ride—
take,
like a dose of medicine.
We take the music cure:
tempos and melodies, vivid
and alive, a salve
late afternoons and evenings.

Take up, take care, take over.

I choose our favorites: Mozart
and Beethoven, Al Hirt and Benny
Goodman, Ella and Louis.

Teresa Brewer and Mercer
Ellington. Dance Hall Days.
Frank Sinatra.

Take to, take time, take back, take it easy.

Sergio Franco's Neapolitan songs.
Bing Crosby—
                        I like the hard-boiled
counterpoint to his sentimental ballads.

Linda Ronstadt, in Spanish.
Her passion and those Latin rhythms
spinning me across the room.

If you take root, you cannot take off

Old Priests and Dotard Presidents

Jesus, will you all lighten up already?
Diagnosis at distance is dangerous!
Forgetting how to say "Anonymous"
In front of a crowd
Does not mean you have dementia
Any more than forgetting
You are a fascist stooge
Makes you a winner
Or any more than
Abusing children for your kicks
Or locking them up away from their folks
Makes you an amoral sinner
If you can just
Forgive yourself
Forget what you've done
And build that Wall
You keep talking about
Clutch those rosary beads
And the Body of Christ
That you love . . .
Hang onto your lovely
Thinning hair . . .
Confess.
All will indeed
Be well.
Forget about it.

Terra Incognita

She studies my face for a sign,
a greeting to alert her
to where she is in space,
how she fits into the orbit of today,

her clothes too big
the world too fast
reality too elusive—
my hand lights on a

morning glory of purple that
flowered on her arm
since last visit,
A Rorschach of dried blood

beneath skin no thicker than a dragonfly wing.
If I look long enough
I may see straight through
to chambered bone

or nerves tinged scarlet,
wrapped around highways of blue—
she is the Lucite model
from my third grade Christmas list,

The Visible Woman marked with four stars,
the highest magnitude of want,
a see-through shell of parts
color-coded for easy identification,

It never landed under the tree,
Malibu Barbie showed up instead,
the cartography of the body
still inscrutable as runes.

99 Ways to Skin A Monkey

Clouds of grief and guilt
enslaved to nowhere a
piece of meat crawling
with flies and maggots

Cocaine strippers and
pole trippers in the canal
brothels of Amsterdam
snow lives on mountains

Rattlesnake owls shaking
feathers in the mesquite
writing the devil's obituary
woven unreality seeing

What cannot be seen
holding hands with the
ghost of the shaman wind
maybe dementia is a dream?

Larry Schulte

Kasoundra's Final Bells

What do the cows think? You rubbing their cowbells with super balls, creating death moan overtones. Cats crying, or alley love. Kasoundra thinks you should lie down on Stage 4, surrounded by octaves of cows. Soprano herefords, alto angus, Charolais bass. You are partial to Holstein tenors, a connection engendered from milking by hand, morning and night, for years. Each cow bends down when their pitch is called for, so your magic can stroke their bells.

Carrie Ann

She was my wildest friend, shocking me
with her uninhibited ways, sailing
into situations without an ounce of restraint,
then laughing her way back out.

Now she has a vagueness around her
as though she's wrapped in mist.
Her words eke out slowly when I lead her with a question.
Without a question,
she sits silent.

I search her face for a trace of the old Carrie Ann,
the one who loved to say *fuck* in gentle, polite company,
the one who'd show up ripped at 3 a.m. and throw herself down
on my living room couch,
the one who tracked down beauty wherever it existed—
in the mountains,
in art galleries,
in old *tiendas* that no one else seemed to know about.
She had the eye, and a wild creativity
that always drew me back for more,
despite her rude ways.

I miss her now.
She's here, but it's just the impenetrable
Buddha-like body sitting next to me.
The flames that once seared
have been snuffed out.

Mary McGinnis

Isabelle

1.
inside her the
song still plays.
among muffled voices, it's hard to
be bold; limited
energy wasted on
logic-defying TV dribble, and
long nights which fail to rest
each eye.

2.
we both remember
our summer mountain picnic–
green fresh air and trees

3.
her goodbye by phone
a soft purr and a meow
from a charming old cat

ANOTHER TUESDAY

Her hands knit and unknit
the crinkling white.
The instant my eyes shift
to the open wings of my journal,
she slides her diaper down more.
"Mimi," I sigh, "don't take that off."
Her hands retreat beneath the sheet,
but there's no stopping her.

Brown sunspots cover
the branching blue backs of her hands,
again they bunch and unbunch
the white handfuls. This is their job—
to fashion her escape.
"Mimi. Stop. Please."
I yank down her brown t-shirt,
stretch it to dress length,
her fingers hide themselves
beneath her thighs.
I tighten the sheet on each side
into an attempted restraint.

Maybe, if they cannot escape instantly,
her hands will forget their task.
Next door, the *squeak-squeak-squeak*
of a nurse's earth shoes.
I hope for them to retreat.
I won't let her to catch
my Mimi this way.

The white plastic bin
sprouts yesterday's *Globe*,
I set it atop Mimi's lap,

44

hope to distract her with that.
For now, she rips strip after strip.
My backpack's zipper echoes
over all that ripping.
I kiss her dry forehead.
She works her lips but
her eyes stay closed.
I ease the door open, check back—
she's already tugging the diaper back down.
"Luv you," I announce to the hall.
Across the shining squares,
my sneakers do not squeak.

She'll slide that damn
diaper down past her ankles,
kick it off before
I sign out and step into the rain—
or surely by the time I've finished
hunting for my lost car,
parked somewhere

Regret

This morning I regret
not going to her house,
not sitting down to hear
stories of her keepsakes
tightly wrapped
and tucked away.

This morning I regret
not calling her when
she was well, before
the cancer battened her down,
ravaging her senses,
wrecking her memory.

That my stories of her
are tamped down
with sorrow, enough
to stop me in my tracks.

She kept herself
so tightly wracked,
carnage of her beauty,
loss of all she treasured.

My Mother's Hands

I.
Her hands were so damaged from housework I could hear the hard jagged skin that edged the splits on her fingertips snag my sweater as she buttoned it under my chin on cool mornings.

II.
When I was older she put the little ones to bed and sat at her loom weaving night music. Heddles, the long hanging needles threaded with warp yarn, tinkled against each other. The harnesses that held the heddles rattled up and down. She threw the shuttle with a deft snap. It slid through the shed of taut warp threads, buzzing along the slotted beater, laying down one more shot of weft. Then she played one or two bass notes by reaching out to flick the sturdy comb-like beater toward her, thumping the new weft into fabric. While her feet pressed the harness pedals, my mother's hands swam like quick dreamers from shuttle to beater and yet found quarter notes in time to stretch and smooth the finished cloth. I often fell asleep listening.

III.

> Alzheimer's
> plucking threads from fabrics
> then smoothing

May Urges Never Cease

Mom and I walk slowly across the street to the fitness center.
She's wrapped in the new hot pink terry cloth robe.

A few exercises, stretches and slogs through the cool pool,
then I help her up the submerged staircase to our towels.

Armed, she walks over to a young, muscular, tattooed guy
with a shaved head, asks him if she can help dry off his back.

Quite puzzled, stunned, really, he quietly refuses.
No, no, she protests, I really can use my towel to get you dry.

Dripping pool water, I dig for my cell phone, call my brother
who lives nearby: I'm biting my cheeks to keep down

a nascent, uncontrollable laugh: *Marty, we must never leave
Mom alone, especially among bare-chested men in swim suits.*

Caryl McHarney

Her Chimayo Jacket

Thou shalt not covet thy mother-in-law's vintage jacket.
Oh, but I secretly do: tailored Chimayo blanket on cedar in the guest-
room closet.

The red wool sleeve says, "touch me." The
sterling silver buttons boast, "we're older than you."

She helps me try it on, smoothing the yoke and back.
Heavy wool wonders if I can bear its weight.

Two square pockets hide promises and candy wrappers.
One red collar turns up its tongue, murmering secrets.

"My uncle bought this for me," she says. "I felt so proud in it!
Father would not let me wear it to church."

Now her jacket comes home to New Mexico with me
retracing the lines of its design.

*   *   *

Years later, on dementia's doorstep
she recalls the jacket but loses the thread.

The 1940s. She travels with her parents—
Route 66 from Kansas to California via New Mexico.

In the dusty trading post, the woven jacket
draws her deeper into its warp and weft.

50

On her 88th birthday, she sat with her knitting in her lap, a small ball of dull yellow feeding into a small square four by four inches on her needles. She had just finished talking to her sister who she thought was her daughter as her daughter who she thought was her sister sat across the room from her. She had been crying, the layers of defense long gone, skin of her heart open almost to the air, so tender

She held
up

of grey

"I'll be starting this one next, it's silver, you know, and when it's gone I'll be dead," I smiled and said, "How mythological!" which startled her, she was not expecting that response, "No," she stammered, she seemed to think I had misunderstood her, "I mean it, I'll be gone." I said "Well, what about the other one?" and pointed to a second slightly smaller ball of grey yarn, "What about that one?" She looked and saw it and laughed and then pretended to be angry. "Well, I can go whenever I want, I don't have to stay." I said "Yes, this is true, you can, you don't have to stay for anyone. I love you."

Another Time, Another Country

All they have is the pure impulse to eat. . .
Carol Muske-Dukes

There's an element of impulse calling
from the candy bowls, soda bottles,
cookie jars, and cakes on the counter.
Graze free now, and constantly. Enjoy.
What can I get you, she asks again.

There. That's the quirk I don't get.
If we're not chewing, she's unhappy
in some place rooted in her — where?
Soul? Heart? Maybe psyche and history.
Where does impulse hide compulsion?

I'll never map the landscape. It just is.
A child of immigrants, deserted wife,
she's never talked about the past hurts.
Now she can't remember yesterday,
leaving bowls of past forever empty.

Ed's Last Dream House

Without warning, the rooms rearrange themselves and locate their furniture elsewhere, create booby traps for the unwary. An unfamiliar hanger in the closet steals your best coat. House plants brush against your cheek to ask for water.

In the middle of the night, you awake without boots in a new jungle. The enemy is storming the camp, and your only weapon is a gnarled walking stick. You use it to smash out the lights so they cannot find you. The broken glass cuts your feet.

In the morning, you relieve yourself in the china chamber pot that has always been under the bed. You found it yesterday in the basement, where for some strange reason your children had hidden it.

If only the Farmer's Almanac calendar on the wall would stop flipping its pages back and forth, forth and back. If only the hands of the mantel clock would not insist on spinning around ahead of the chime or in back of the hour, you would know perfectly well what day it is, what time, why it is suddenly important to everyone around you that you remember this day, this hour, as opposed to a happy remembrance of your own choosing.

You have plans. You will rebuild the house with firmer walls that do not dissolve in mist when you want to hang a picture, with doors that no longer open to foreign landscapes. But to the front walk lined with lily-of-the-valley. To the back screened porch overcome with the heavy, familiar scent of lilacs.

53

Linda Flaherty Haltmaier

The Upside of Dementia

She ate a cookie that wasn't there,
brought it to her lips and
bit down with the certainty
of a guillotine,
she chewed
bit again
stared off—
I asked how it tasted,
this magical cookie—
Delicious, just delicious,
would you like one, Honey?
Her hand came to rest on her lap,
quaking slightly,
invisible cookie held tight.

Karen Downs-Barton

The Waning Summer

Invisible thread
the fly, silk swaddled, twirls
a liquefying last waltz

Under the parasol / geisha white you sit / talking // soft cirrus
clouds of hair / brush your face // compartmentalised
conversations / without connections / drifting // our minds
wander / to questions / touching your arm / the skin / wafer
thin // what is the paper / in cupboards / drawers // the breeze
shifts // Papier d'Armenie / such a pretty name / you say it
so well / is it scenting still / under clothes // my answers
unheeded // a bird alights / head cocked / a soft silence
between / alluvial meanderings // question / your friendly lacuna
who are you // gone / the black sheep / the daughter / names
barriers // each time / we talk / your gentle joy / at revelations /
compensations I bask in / I am a poet / we're best friends //

Evening. A late damask rose drops
Furling
kisses

Lisa's Now

Waves wash over her stretch of sand
erasing the tracings of yesterday
my colorsketch of our tomorrow
dissolves in background of blackness

no black can taint the *now* hidden in her
treasures from daybreak's earnest quest
stones in moondust chokeberry goldenrod
blessings of the wild for morning's table

daily drive to Harkness Park marked with
look another copper   that's eight or is it six
beeches maples color siblings re-re-tallied
with her wish to eavesdrop on their gossip

park peninsula we christened cathedral
God in copper beeches brushing clouds
whisperings of the Spirit borne by breezes
over waters of the Sound that surround us

as I mourn a dying dogwood she hits me
with *see that branch how many leaves still alive*
on cue storm clouds appear to part for her
to catch the smallest patch of heavenblue

Harkness done her *let's come back again*
comes with clutch of clover dandelion
buttercup tucked in a fan leaf of gingko
quiet grace for end table's tiny vase

sunset her porchtime apart no time
for mind or memory solely for soul
colors blooming blending deepening
washing over blues of a skyscape

chamber concert shutters the day
ignored composers on our CD playlist
Carl Nielsen Amy Beach rise to the top
so
    lights
        hush

slipping toward sleep time once more for
what brought me from Austria   *how long*
are we together   *oh my so many many years*
drifting hand on palm we're gone as one.

The Value of Knowledge

Nelson knows a lot, more than many,
about the Chosin Reservoir,
about December of 1950.
He's there now, once more, again,
on this May afternoon,
this unseasonably hot,
deceivingly beautiful day
in a commuter suburb of Chicago.

> *Today we will study Korea, children.*
> *The South is our friend,*
> *the North no one's comrade.*
> *Yes, I know: Love one another.*
> *Please don't ever forget those words,*
> *even if you remember nothing else.*
> *I've brought you some kimchi fried rice,*
> *some Binggrae banana milk:*
> *You'll recognize the taste,*
> *but likely not the mix of Hanja and Hangul*
> *wrapped around the bottle.*

Nelson doesn't know about missing toes,
the phantom strike of midnight pain
mimicking frostbite in a fool's sunshine
that won't stop fresh piss from icing.
He doesn't know about missing friends,
their not waking in the snow,
them not getting up after the sniper,
the artillery round, the soulless cold.
In the world he occupies right now,
despite the presence of family right here,
these things are only beginning.

58

Today, at recess, you will not fear the airplanes
coming to O'Hare and Midway;
we'll study him and there another time.
You won't think twice, perhaps not once,
about the backfire and rattle of a truck.
Until then, please pay attention.
These are lessons Nelson wrote for you.
If you get drowsy on this fine May day,
I promise not to slam my hand,
surely not the classroom yardstick,
on the surface of your desk.

Janet Eigner

The Daughter's Instruction
Me: (a greenhorn at a constructive
dementia chat):

Mom and I board the memory unit's tour bus,
a trip through the rural green hills of San Diego.

Mom: *Janet, Cousin Doris invited us for lunch.*

Janet: But mom, Cousin Doris lived in Chicago.
        Didn't she pass away some years ago?

Mom: No, I'm quite sure she invited us.

Me: We take in the scrubgrass, Indian casino,
      a warm silence between us.
      Twenty minutes pass.

Mom*: Janet, I just heard from cousin Doris—*
      today isn't a good time for us
      to visit her for lunch.

Me: Well darn! Lunch won't be the same
       without Cousin Doris at Sllvergate.

60

Lauren Camp

Is Empty He Says

Every two weeks I ache
in his conversations his breakable
stories his word-spelling the useless sticky
ways he repeats what he knew
and then his numbers
incomplete but ticking how
they enchant and pass
through many times
I stood I stand
by the toaster and listen
to the smell of his blinkings
his voice still
music and the clear echoing
and the cup empties and the cup
is empty he says goodbye
eight ways says he is guided and I am full
of the last line next word the scorch
of fortune his unhappy leanings
and then he transposes nouns the days
narrow not belonging and I listen but know
nothing the phone line dead

Shirley Blackwell

Sound Bound

I rise with birds of dawn, to seek the solitary hour
sanity craves before the daily sentence starts again.
I hear the whispered hope of steam in kettle,
bubbles rock against the stainless steel.

The tea is scalding in my cup.
High in my nose, I taste its fresh perfume,
It is criminal to forsake its silken bergamot
so soon to brew the black, strong coffee
the ancient crone, now my obligation,
learned to drink on graveyard at the depot.

Even now the brew, with a night of sleep,
gives her, for an hour or so, a cogent mind
and something of her memory of old.

I cling to this aria of peace, which briefly plays
until another theme creeps in—
discordant percussions are the herald
of beginning and of end—
shuffle flop of slippers, fleece-lined feet on tile
shut-shut, shut-shut shut-shut.

Break of day or a sense of those astir
has roused her from her bed.
The scuff of sound warns of her approach.
Shut-shut and I stoop out of sight,
knowing that her failing ears
can't record my guilty flight.

Too soon, I must play warden,

invoke the vigilant eye;
keep her car keys high, out of her reach,
give plausible excuse, reasons for delay
in letting her return to live alone
in the home she's known for fifty years
her sanctuary, where she is no longer safe.

With Doeppler finely tuned to the juggernaut
shut-shut, shut-shut, shut-shut,
chugging without letup toward my day,
I once more steel myself to play
out our mutual sentence. How long
will I serve as jailer, fugitive, and
prisoner—here, in my own home?

Dorothy Alexander

Sibyl's Question

Which one of the girls am I?
she asks, imploring eyes
searching her child's face.

Her daughter, who never says
the word Alzheimer out loud
struggles to answer, is struck
dumb with a sudden
vision of the future.

Mother Losing Her Mind

When my mother started losing her mind
she couldn't remember the people

in her photo albums which was a blessing
because most of them had died.

She wasn't sure how she hurt herself
but seeing blood was frightening.

She couldn't stop looking for her car keys
even though she couldn't drive.

When we moved her to assisted living
one by one her children's faces departed.

She allowed her body to surrender to gravity
and slowly sank into the deep end.

She began to walk in short steps, like a Geisha,
then she forgot how to walk.

One day my mother couldn't remember
how to eat,

she stared at the food on her plate
and wondered what the fork was for.

Today, my mother is content,
she sits in her wheelchair and stares,

she surrounds herself in silence.
All she is is now.

Assisted Living

My mother
        lives among
                strangers now
      people who don't know
           her open
                generous
                      broken
                            spirit.

I worry
        she is seen
                as an object
                    rather than a person.

I don't care how
        vacated her body and mind appear,
                new traumas
      will imprint
                upon her soul
                    in the same proportion
      as they may
                upon her body.

I wish she was with people
who love her and know her.
        Where are her glasses?

Carved Out Of Dizzy

Clogged ears and eyes
a chemical confusion—
rough time sleeping,
very cold hands, even pajamas hanging loose; is she
dying? "Take whatever you want

out of my house: the carpet, the
undercarpet . . ." Just
two months ago, she suggested we

order in lunch,
fantasized us coming over for quiche. Some days slightly

dizzy with confusion—
"I think she needs more protein," we all said, we put her
zigzag paintings on her wall and also said, "without the zig-zag walker,
you might fall down." We don't know what to do.

Auntie B

she pampered me
with kind words,
and baby talk,

pinched my cheeks
told me to smile,
showed me how
by pushing up the corners
of my mouth.

Her own smile
was slightly insincere,
yet honest.
She pitied my poverty
and father's absence.

She suffered
what no women should—
the loss of two boys
a heartbeat from being men,

and her husband had cancer
when their plan was
he would
take care of her

Addiction to pills
and obesity became her
visible disease,

making the end, more sour
than sweet. Her daughter
attended to her needs.

Auntie B was confused,
impatient, in pain;
but otherwise in good cheer

in front of others
(except the help)
whom she abused with words
ran off.

What next? Of course
her daughter placed her
in a nursing home

where she heard and saw
two lovers having sex
in an empty room
(imagined)

and smeared her feces
on the wall--
her common sense gone,
grace replaced
by human indignity,
embraced madly.
In her great final pain
she asked her daughter to catch the baby
she believed she was giving birth to.

Later, her daughter smiled and said,
"I guess that would be me."

Caregiver
—for my mother

For a while she could prop him up
provide appearance of normalcy
like the poles, guy lines, and pegs of a tent
that hold up
an increasingly brittle exterior
protect what is becoming
— emptiness —

        answer the repeated question again . . .
        . . . repeated question again . . .

        calm his agitated insistence that he, long retired
        had to go to work

        rescue him from a never-ending gyre
        of tooth-brushing, hair-combing, and face-washing
        in the middle of the night, bring him back to bed

        let his angry stubbornness roll off her shoulders

        clean him up in the bathroom

        watch ballgames on TV—
        even though she didn't like sports—until
        he no longer understood the rules
        what once brought joy—now bewilderment

        take him to church, constantly watch
        facilitate conversations

        catch him when he falls

even when it means they both fall

make things familiar, predictable, soothing
in his increasingly fragmented world

refuse to put him in a nursing home
resist getting home care help
bear up, put on a positive face
be strong, smile
get a little sleep
do it again . . .
. . . *every* day

It was her duty and promise as a wife
she had said the words—
for better, for worse, in sickness and health—
she meant them
she intended to keep the commitment
she could do this

It was only after—
relief and exhaustion beyond grief and loss—
that we really knew what she had done

Shirley Blackwell

Pardon

I wed her son, sought to be daughter,
but I soon discerned the truth;
she was loath to play Naomi,
I, reluctant to be Ruth.

She ruled as if she were a monarch,
with family bowing to demands.
For forty years, I waited, silent,
as she issued her commands.

Now I tell her, "Put your coat on.
Come this way. Sit down and eat."
To her, these words spell insurrection,
to me, a charge that I must keep.

Sight and hearing (ninety years' worth)
dimming now, but what's unkind
above all else is the unwinding
of a once bright, nimble mind.

In God's mercy, what's the reason
that she must live on in pain,
without eyes, ears, understanding?
What's the lesson to be gained?

Are these years a purgatory
meant for her—or meant for me—
to learn compassion, forsake rancor,
find the path to amity?

At the start, I burned in anger;
slowly, my heart's turned toward trust.
So, she'll go with my true blessing
when her dust returns to dust.

Dementia

"You look just like my daughter," my mother says to me.
"I am your daughter," I tell her.
"You're not a little girl anymore?" she asks.
"No, not for a long time now."

"I have a secret," she says.
"What is your secret?" I ask her.
She leans in and whispers in my ear,
"I'm younger than you'll ever be."

Rina Ferrarelli

Second Wife?

I'm reading, cutting a clipping or two
of time, a space for myself, when I hear
the floor upstairs creaking, the steps.
It's eleven at night, I say, *what
are you doing dressed to go out?*

*I saw the light and decided to come down.
I want to talk.* I wonder if he's awake
or still in some kind of dream. *I know
we've been together for a while now,
about three years or so. . . right? but how*

did we meet? I can't seem to remember.
Daughter, sister, second wife? Once more
I explain how we met, who we were when
we met, who we are now or seem to be.

Memento Mori

I let my father have his mad. His mouth
against death. *Is forgetting a crime?* He censors
every blurred paradigm and what holds
repeats. Never a reflexive
reason when you noodle in Alzheimer's.
Everything cruel, crucial.

I said a final yes
to the counselor and coiled

my answers. Yes, I will truth the depth
of his failing, then return
to talking the weather. I no longer think
a body is shelter. Outside, cobwebs
in the roses, sheets of crows and the sun remains
frantic. Turning and turning.

Jim Ransom

At Riverwalk

I think to ask, "Do you know who I am?"
She studies me with anxious eyes, and then,
Cautiously, "I do, you're my brother, Jim."

She sits and watches intently as I
Chatter on about this and that, hoping
To spark memory behind the question mark

in her fixed gaze. I mention home and she
Is moved to speak, "My mother ..." and then
Perplexed, apologetic, "I forget."

I lean in to kiss her withered cheek,
"Not to worry," baffled by the silence
Into which my words so haplessly reach.

She smiles shyly, shrugging her thin shoulders,
Then slowly turns her head to stare across
The wide relentless river sliding by.

To a Demented Professor

(to late Prof. Sasthri of Bapatla Engineering College)

"Professor of computer engineering or…"
he introduces himself to a handful of humans,
trying to shoo away a pair of bitches playfully
snarling over a ragged slipper at the college gates.

Those stately constructions of a
so-called communal strength and
an elemental glow in a granite attire
are deceptive adornments of beauty

some nostalgic wounds, mock him
but are "only like a fragment
in the scrap heap beside my bed
unwanted as myself" he mocks.

A flock of pigeons explode the
hope of a reappointment into a
great flutter nostalgically echoing
in the department of civil engineering

but deaf-eared to his gabbles
about some blues of deprivation,
while he asks for a rupee or two.
Does that annoy? A pity!

On the last visit to ours invited me home
and Proclaimed: "There was a time dear boy
I was revered for mobilizing funds.
They owe a lot for my yeoman's service,"

78

suddenly rummaged through crumpled dailies,
leaned on me saying, "You should be a sub-editor
boy for *Bharat-Bhoomi* —My dream magazine. I will
scandalize those notorious landlords (*chaudaris*)."

A curtain of twilight counts
the autumn years of senility
shading the halo of knowledge
and the slippers bears his cross.

"Great delegates will throng to my funeral
with heavy hearts and newspaper profiles
on me will shame my students." Went on…
oblivious of the half-sipped tea of life.

A post-waiting-for-Godot existentialist?
An unlucky Pozo or Lucky?
A manifestation of identity in an irredeemable exile?
Suddenly clouds swarm and vanish

taking away the elemental hope from him
leaving only a storm in his half sipped teacup
An embarrassed Mrs. Shastri avoids visitors.
Occasionally a train hoots a presage of some death.

Visiting Mother

Her hands close and pull at the air just inches from my neck. She reaches for long strands but I've cut my hair short. She knows me from somewhere but that was a lifetime ago. She takes my hand in both of hers. Her hands are wrinkled, her skin is thin and her veins are blue. She searches my eyes, trying to place me. I ask her if she likes living in this place. She says she is worried about lunch.

We pass a piano on the way to the cafeteria where she stops to gaze at the keys. I know by her face that her hands remember. She tells me about dances that she used to go to with her husband. His name is Ken. Every man she dances with is Ken. Ken is every man she ever married and every man she dreams about. She points to a resident shuffling down the hall. There he goes my mother says, that's my Ken, and she follows him.

Karen Petersen

Parkinson's Persona

My husband is really bad tonight.
I can take the insults, but not
the hitting and slapping.
And when he decides
to look for a baseball bat
to beat me with, hard,
it is too much.
I told my son who lives with us
his father can be his ward now:
I'm done.
Do you hear me?
I went upstairs to listen to music
and I knew he'd follow me up
because he hadn't finished insulting me.
So now he's in bed, yelling,
and I pray he will become exhausted
and go to sleep, the tantrums over.
I will sit in silence
and stare at the bright moving shadows
from the flickering night light
imagining that
there must be a way through this
but love is not enough.

Kathy Lundy Derengowski

Remember Please

Forgive me if I should forget
My purse, or where I left my car
I know that they're important yet
I can't remember where they are.

I make my lists to help me so
I will recall my every chore
I lose those lists. It seems as though
They do not help much anymore.

I know that I repeat too much
The same old stories day to day
I know that I seem out of touch
That sometimes I am in your way.

Now that my time is almost through
I pray you will think well of me.
If I could ask one thing of you—
Remember who I used to be.

Just yesterday you came to call
We visited, you spent the day
By evening I forgot it all
Another moment slipped away

Though thoughts grow dim, though I can't see
Or think to look ahead and plan
While there are days still left to me
I'll live each hour the best I can.

While age has had an awful cost
In things that I am frightened of
For all the treasures I have lost
I'm blessed, for I remember...love.

Parallel Universe

1

The rubber ducks cried for me last night.
I could not remember my Nursery Rhymes,
intimate friends in childhood.
Where have they gone?
I press lips against stone,
neither see nor hear my past.
Something within is leaving
me naked and bare. A suppressed scream,
disguised denial. I could become my mother.
Sudoku, scrabble, the daily crossword.
Will any of them come to save me?
Learn to play an instrument.
Learn a new language.
Everyone has a piece of advice, no one an answer.
Why can't I fade into the universe
and take jackrabbit with me?
His big floppy ears my alarm.
His speed my getaway car.
Running and hiding does not work.
Karma bites your butt no matter where you hide.

2

Mama's head told her she took a bath today.
Mama's head told her she took her medicine today.
Mama's head told her the lady down the hall stole her bedspread.
Mama's head told her she had 4 roommates and they all left.
None of these things are true. How do you compete with
Mama's head when all the synapses that define reason
retired and abandoned Mama at the bus stop. But Mama still gives
orders as if perfectly normal.

84

3
Mama left a few years ago
Don't know where she went.
She tries to visit her body sometimes
and you always turn her away.
You took over and nobody can get through.
You have stolen the deeds to her temple.
Mama and I would like to know your plans.

4
The doctors place chips on the roulette wheel
at name brand locations: Aricept and Namenda.
Scientists released only the short report. The final verdict
still rides the waves. Mama and I don't have that much time.
Perhaps a future generation will catch a healing wave
and drown you at sea wicked Alzheimer.

The Rich Tapestry

We weave slowly,
recapturing strands of memories you
lost. Our loom a journal where strands
of yesterdays slow shuttle from my pen.
Your hesitant warps gain shots of unexpected
colour. The scent of mown grass teases
thoughts of green gloves, once owned
and we sewed them to the page
in tendrils of verdant ink.
A spoon of yoghurt recalls a snowman
someone built; perhaps a lover you never
revealed. A picture saved from our fridge gallery
is appliquéd lovingly to a waiting page.
Some images are lost to time.
The hammer you could not name
we shut it away in a box.
But the fear of not knowing
somehow stitched itself on to our canvas,
drew your eyes to its sarcophagus long after
the unnamed thing it contained was itself
forgotten. And like an eclipse of moths
it ate holes in the safety
of our memory blanket.

Conversation with Mom, Labor Day, 2010

Mom: Janet? When did you call?
Mom: How are you, Janet?
J: I'm feeling well, walking a couple of miles, pain free, every day now.
Mom: A couple of little...uh, oh, what am I saying?
The wheel, I waited too long, it went off a little longer than I wanted it to;
I'll just wait until the wheel peels off and then we'll both be healed and ok.
J: The wheel? Do you mean the wheel of life or the wheel on your walker or what?
Mom: Yes, uh huh. Then we'll both be ok.

Mary Strong Jackson

You Don't Understand I'm in a Jam

I wander through my parent's home of the past 30 years, packing dad's things for the nursing home. The sense of my mother being gone is stronger, as if an already dead person can seem more gone, but she does. I know which shirts she'd want me to choose for him, and seeing the stick pins all over the United States map showing all the places dad hauled farm machinery from East to West Coast makes the end of their lives together more visible and painful. This feels like dropping your last child off for kindergarten, but instead of a new beginning, it is the beginning of an end.

I carry his things into the Valley Care Facility, walk into his room, and see an old man sitting in a chair. He wasn't this old last month. I note a new softness filling his body and mind. His metamorphosis feels disorienting. I see my hard-drinking, truck-driving, fist-fighting father become mellow, accept others making choices for him, and need me more than he'd ever admitted.

I fill out the social history paperwork for the nursing home. I check nothing under hobbies but write, "he liked to watch old movies, old Westerns, but not anymore." My sister said you could have added,

"He likes to drink, dance, and get in bar fights". Even that behavior was years ago.

Dad opens his eyes. He has trouble finding words, so talking with him means playing a word association game. He makes connections like calling his room a cabin. Who wouldn't want their tiny, shared nursing home room to be a cabin?

"The donkey we had for dinner yesterday was not good, but lunch today tasted better," Dad says. He's been reporting the various kinds of meat he's been eating, and he calls them by the animal, so beef is cow, and pork is pig, but he has also mentioned squirrel, monkey, and duck.

"How's mom?" he asks. "I saw her, but another lady is using her name."

"Mom died two years ago," I say. "Someone's using the name Ruth Jackson?"

"I know she died. Yes, I didn't know that happens. That they would do that."

"Use other people's names?" I ask.

"Well, that they shear a person like a sheep when they put them in the casket."

"Hmmm," I nod.

"I talked to your sister Babe. She said to say 'hello' and she'll try and see you soon. Babe always took good care of you, didn't she? She looked out for you when you were little."

"Yes, she did." His chin shook, and tears run down his cheeks. I put my hand on his arm. Tears run down my cheeks. I'd seen my dad cry only a few times—when he was ill in the hospital and scared, when mom died, and now.

"I wish I could live by a river."

"Me too, Dad. I've always wanted to live near water."

Day 4 in the Nursing Home:

I type into Google:

"life expectancy of 81-year-old man with dementia and untreated non-Hodgkin's lymphoma"

"average length of stay by nursing home residents"

"life expectancy of 81-year-old man who sees dead relatives"

"old man with dementia in a nursing home with ungodly long toenails, sees dead relatives—sees his dead mother and the dead brother he liked better than the other also dead brother, and he asks his daughter to wheel him around the nursing home to find Brother Fred and their mother. He worries his mom is not being taken care of." Of course, no help there. I don't want him to suffer, but I know his days are not always comfortable. Or am I wanting to know how long I have to watch my dad's downhill journey?

Later, "Can you put me in your car, take me home? I am in a jam."

"It's a new place, and you haven't been here long, so it's not surprising you feel confused."

"You don't understand. I've always been able to get myself out of anywhere." These might be the most honest words my dad ever said to me.

90

I feed him chocolate pudding with whipped cream, and he says, "Mmmm" with every bite. He hadn't lost his sweet tooth, it would be his last taste of sweetness.

"I'm going home now, dad."

"Don't forget I'm here."

"I won't ever forget you are here."

"I thought you did last week," he says.

"I won't forget, and I promise I'll see you tomorrow."

Postlude

All agreed it was a blessing,
gave thanks that, when it arrived,
it was peaceful and swift.
Heart ruled over head, at last,
foiling dementia's cruel slide.

A life and all its seasons
celebrated with full honors,
and the guilt for wishing that
her body not survive
her mind's demise
will diminish,
given time and reason.

The courtesies are done,
thanks said to the proper people,
forms and rites fulfilled,
phone calls of appreciation,
all required notifications.

Where there was
hypervigilance and stress
there is now an easing
of tight shoulders, grief
softened by relief,
gratitude for grace,
but not yet self-forgiveness.

We focus on tasks
that must be done
by those still living.
We pass her empty room,
silently sidestepping her absence,
which persists at every turn.

Dostoyevsky and Pajamas

*For the mystery of human existence lies not in just
staying alive, but in finding something to live for.*
—from *The Brothers Karamazov*

He wonders.
How did I lose my balance?
When did time pass without my knowing?
Why did I let this happen?

He used to walk unaided, on toes and heels.
When did he succumb to wheels?
How did his ears grow plastic inserts
with tiny filaments and switches?
Why did he exchange Dostoyevsky for *Jeopardy*?

When did his vision deteriorate and membranes dry—
scheduled tears dropped in
or eyes watering at random?
How did his bladder become a drainage bag?
Why has his voice declined?
When did his caregiver become his conscience
reminding him to drink more water, take a nap, and shave?

Each night, he loosens time from his wrist
removes his second set of eyes
places his ears in their container
and his spare teeth
in their cup. He slides off his slippers,
releases his stable grip.

Other hands take over.
They put him in his pajamas,
adjust his pillows,
and tuck him into bed.
After the nightly tears are dropped in,
he closes his eyes,
freed from his own Grand Inquisition
of hows and whens and whys.
He alternately sleeps and wakes
and dreams of another tomorrow
that never come.

A Touched Life

Lunch under a chalk map; a quiet welcome
parting in silence. Raw textures better than
line drawings. The balance of luminosity
shivering in a ravished region.

Grand jewels fertilize danger.
Fearful slumber frozen in ruin.
A storm starved and developed
in vice.

Solar winds warp into communal heights.
The autumn sprawl of pigmented desperation.
The winds do not rein in world efforts
at spastic needs. It's elastic middle slowly
deviates into a drastic obsolete space.
Prevailing is a tendency toward a sullen
reverence. Short winds, like musical notes,
wrap and raise uneasily over gulf tidal
movement. Bolts of exotic winds contort
like long fingers under the strain of
arthritis. Wind stays sleepless in the
hidden quality of evil.

When I was fragile in the vast frothy world,
angles tangled me in disregard, placed tags
on my limbs, and left me in empty lots to
lean on drafty construction site detritus.
These vivid memories are tucked into
shards for novels, as are tumors of invisible
flesh.

Clueless

My dad suffered from
obsessive compulsive disorder,
frantically searched for elusive names
of things, places, people.

When fleeting labels slipped away,
he fussed until they could be recovered,
worried he was losing his mind,
like my grandfather who developed dementia.

After his death, mom discovered
shoeboxes filled with paper scraps
containing his handwritten notes,
words finally remembered.

I sympathize, share his feverish need
to capture language, metaphoric clues
that lead from mute torment
to meaningful communication.

Anne M. Shaughnessy

ANY SOOTHING WHISPER

My father's mind turned to mud.
     He couldn't recall
the color of his own toothbrush,
     but he remembered
soft swears from 80 years past,
     the floodwater's final stink.
Grey diluvial muck
     blanketed the basement,
eons it took to clean up,
     raw-knuckled days
beside my tired grandmother,
     They scrubbed the silt-crusted coal,
his forearms a solid ache,
     her knees utterly stove up.
She who never swore
     cursed that sink's solid black.
"It's all right, Mum,"
     my four-year-old father cooed.
Now any black crescent fingernail,
     any soothing whisper,
tears him back through time.

Multi-tasking

My Grandmother
looks at me
and continues our conversation.
Turns another page
of the book she is reading,
flips over another card,
winning the solitaire game
she is playing.

I marvel.

Years later, I call her
at her final home.
In her meanderings
she takes me for
an older sister I never had.
She tells me
her words won't work.

Sylvia Ramos Cruz

That Wall

*In Albuquerque, hard to believe, sometimes
the rain comes down on one side of the road
and not the other, and, if you're fast, you can
keep dry by running to the sunny side.*

Today it's raining hard in my yard,
only on the west side of my yard.
Up and down along 7-foot-tall wall
warped pieces of wood, trash,
bricks and cinder blocks
fly, thud, plop, crunch on gravel,
oleander, prized Camaro.

My neighbor, Hal, has lost his mind;
can no longer find his way
to the bin across the street, so he lobs
daily refuse and years of yard accumulations
like offerings to the heavens
which, he must figure, are due east.

Perched on a ladder, I spy on him
over my side of the wall—thinning,
yet still wiry body, no shirt, no shoes—
on a hot-as-hell day. I say, *Hal you need
to cover up or you'll burn.* He doesn't
seem to think this fencely apparition strange,
though peers at me puzzled for a bit, then says
he just came out to do some work. I say,
Please don't throw trash into my yard.
I don't, he says. *I have pictures,* I reply.
Pictures are nothing, he lets fly.

Climbing down I wonder if he means
he doesn't care that I have picture evidence.
Or that pictures are not real. Or that he
no longer has pictures in his head.
It's hard to know
when someone is on the other side
of that wall.

Distraction

We've had to lie to my Mother,
my sister and I,
in order to transition her into assisted living.
She has a touch of dementia
and can't be left alone.
The years of 24/7 home care
have diminished her funds substantially.
The story we told her
is that a water pipe broke in the wall,
flooding her house.
The damage will take months to clean up and repair.
"I just want to go home.
I'm sick of hearing that guy moan all night."
She nodded in the direction of her neighbor.
"I don't belong here with all these creepy old farts."
"I know," I tell her, putting my hand on hers.
"If I don't get to go home soon,
I'll die.
I know I will."

Trying to distract her,
I pulled out some photographs from an old Buffums box.
There were several of my stepfather, Steve, when he was young.
"Steve used to screw the waitresses
who worked at that coffee shop he always hung out at."
I looked at her,
my mouth falling open.
"Dad screwed waitresses?"
She laughed.
"Well, not anymore. That was years ago.
Besides, I have no right to be."

She picked up a Polaroid,
studying it with a magnifying glass.
She was dancing with her gardener,
Hector,
his arm around her waist,
her skirt twirling up.
Steve's head didn't make it into the photo,
but I could see his hands lifting
a bare midriff.
A pair of tanned legs in red stilettos
flew in the air.

She threw the photo onto her bed.
I watched her grab the bottle of Merlot
on her nightstand,
pouring it into a crystal goblet
that I had brought from her house.
A voice called "Bingo" from the nearby rec room.
Her hand shook as she lifted the glass,
downing the wine in a couple of gulps.
"I'm not one of them," she said,
pointing at an old man in a wheelchair
rolling by her open door,
mumbling incoherently.
"Goddammit, can't you see I'm not one of them?"

Curtis Hayes

Earl

he's an 81-year-old
son of the Lonestar State,
still standing straight and tall,
his skin dry and cracked by the
Texoma sun.
short-term memory is
scrambled
but his long-term is good.
he asks me where I'm from.

he says he was out in California once,
as a Marine in 1943.
he remembered an earthquake
while he and other recruits
were drilling
out on the parade ground
and his Sargent yelling
"Hit the deck!"
he remembers grabbing
for a hand-hold as
as the Earth shook
but there was nothing
but grass and dirt.
we drink Dr. Pepper
and he asks me where I'm from

he says he was out in California once
in the service
and he once drove down Hollywood Blvd.
where he saw
a man dressed as a woman.

104

"Can you imagine that?
Right there on the street.
I'd never seen anything like it
before or since."
he shakes his head,
still astonished.

Earl's got a new pickup truck
that he's not allowed to drive
anymore
and a wife of 56 years, still pretty,
and still good behind the wheel.

he tells me that he had a misfit uncle
who got mixed up with the Barrows
and ended up shot down
by The Law
and that back then
The Law
wasn't much better
than the crooks in North Texas.
he wipes his freckled head
with a faded red bandana.
he smiles at me
and then he asks me where I'm from.

He Keeps the Gas Tank Full

The old pick-up truck
     has been in the carport for years.
It's an old stick shift
     that his son doesn't wanna drive.
If he's got something to haul,
     he relies on his neighbor to jump that truck.
And still, he keeps the gas tank full.

He takes Fridays off,
     for an ongoing love affair.
She's a rusty old vet,
     on blocks in his buddy's shed.
He's got a case of beer,
     going to the guy who can find that part.
And still, he keeps the gas tank full.

1. I'm free to go.
2. When I decide.
3. It's up to me.
4. My gas tank's full.

He's got a vintage bike,
     that he tinkers with all alone.
He's got every tool,
     and still can't get it to run.
Before he calls it a night,
     he polishes the chrome with an old grease rag.
And still, he keeps the gas tank full.

He sits alone at home,
      in a Lincoln with suicide doors.
He starts up the car,
      folds the top down into the trunk.
With many road trips ahead,
      the state took his license on his birthday.
And still, he keeps the gas tank full.

Fill'er up boys!

Lyrics by Jeanne M. Favret & Virginia "Ginger" Rice
Music by Blane Sloan & Roger Baker

Gracie Panousis

Sunny Plaza

They're sitting lined up along the walls
some in tall white vinyl chairs with wheels
not quite wheelchairs
they can stand and walk in them
but not walkers either, they have seats

Most just sit and look
watch is the wrong word
stare might be better
some turn heads as you pass
most do not

My mother has a new roommate
she is chatty, intelligent, articulate
after a half hour of good conversation she rises
goes to closet and extracts a handbag
pink sweater she casually flings over crooked arm

Gotta go now,
been awfully nice visiting with you
my father needs me
don't wait up
I'll be late

She leaves the room
and moves out into the hall
of the locked Alzheimer's Unit

My mother turns to me
where's she going?
I don't know, she can't leave

108

She's nuts says my mother
who sometimes remembers
where the bathroom is

Sunny Plaza Too

His arm seems always raised in greeting
coming out of the stairwell and turning the corner
the first thing you see are the windows into the
dining room where he sits
wide smile seems
incongruous with the surroundings

The room is a cacophony
of shrieks and colors
all wear long plastic bibs—
chin to waist—
over bright blouses, sweaters, pajama tops,
hospital gowns

Hi Darlin' he calls
George dresses in short-sleeved,
buttoned-down shirts
always carefully tucked
into light chinos
suede house slippers cradle feet
that have carried him for 90 years

Never forgets a name
Shauna, the corn-rowed cocoa-skinned aide
tells me
Watch this, she says

Hey George, you think I'm pretty?
Sure, he beams, thick white hair falling
onto pink forehead
For a colored girl, he answers

She laughs uproariously
winking at me

As I rise to go
I tell him goodbye
He thrusts his hand out to me

I know better
having gone through this before
but step closer anyway
and get pulled into his
desperate embrace
Shauna comes
to help release me

When I leave
I head straight to the mall
and buy things I don't
care about

The Mind is an Eraser

1.
mother would take me birdwatching

she taught me how to focus
to use binoculars to identify birds
by sound

she mostly liked the black birds
they were harder to identify

2.
small black birds took off
one
after another

more birds broke silence
into shards of air

mother could hear them
tiny black berries at this distance

heart misfiring cylinders
inquiring *what is life*

3.
mother is eating bird-like
pecking at rice

(as a child I fed an abandoned baby robin
with an eye-dropper
one squeeze and wait)

I feed my mother drop

by missed drop
as she closes her beak

she forgets what a mouth is for

it is for expressing memory

4.
black birds move awkwardly fighting wind
struggle like my mother

5.
wind off the Gulf Stream is different
Franklin gulls won't challenge those winds

the wind is significantly strong enough
to make their black heads surrender

(the strongest current
is the one in the corridor
bringing gusts of silence
to my mother's mind)

6.
distance traveling between words becomes wider

it is impossible to fly against headwinds
no one takes off in these conditions

brown-headed cowbirds do not risk tiring their wings

mother takes off

7.
in her mind she could be dancing
in a large ballroom
to music not there

at the end is a dot of light
her eyes track

deadness is inside

(a robin-sized rusty blackbird watches
with its pale-yellow eyes
making a *chack* song
like swinging a corroded gate hinge)

mother responds by turning towards the noise
never having seen *this* bird before

9.
once a person slips into a hole
they escape to the other side
as a musical note
from a red-winged blackbird
a liquid burbling
tee-err

10.
the mind is furiously bailing
its canoe from a slow leak
filling faster than buckets can toss
into an endless ocean

(a petite blackish head
Bonaparte's gull
circles above in the loss

makes a nasal *cherr*)

all she has is this bucket
with a gaping hole

11.
(an iridescent-black boat-tailed grackle scolds

in whistles

clucks

then harshly
check
check
check)

    12.
she had been staring at a mirror
for days

no one is there
no one is *home*

a clean slate

(outside, swift speckled eastern starlings scatter as wind
taking their whistled *whoooe* sound with them)

the mirror is dark
shedding feathers

    13.
disappearances come more often
lasting longer
are more profound
more pronounced

after a while
absence becomes permanent
the mind migrates elsewhere
into the *Nowhere*

she misplaces the names of objects
Where did I leave then this time?

(A large hawk-like northern raven alternates flapping
sailing on flat wings
croaking *cr-r-ruck*
with his "Roman-nose" beak)

mother alternates falling and swooping

she squawks
do I know you

(black birds tap on her window)

((a spirit guide?))

14.
when a drop of water lands on paper
it leaves a fingerprint

mother is that drop
leaving no trace

black birds have left for the season
not one snow flake stays

(think how long one drifting snowflake takes
to fall from the sky

that is how long her thoughts take
sometimes never landing)

15.
she had been sitting in the dark
gazing into it
as if she was watching a television show

I wanted to ask
what is it like there

but she was in so deep
there was no turning back

        16.
one day like any other day she went outside
onto the porch
and that is as far as she went

she stood all day in rain until someone moved her
asking her what she was doing
she did not answer or blink or respond

it's as if she had flown away
left her body behind an empty nest
woven with twigs and white hair and twine

they put her away
for her own good
for her own protection

this is when she began escaping

        17.
dates and days
became important to her

I keep saying
it is Wednesday
it is noon

in a lucid moment
she asks
when's the last time we went on a family vacation

I'm guessing
June fifty years ago
anything more precise I can't do

117

18.
(she has been dead over a year now
I can't remember the date
I could look it up
I have a death certificate

I think

I'm not certain
I must be sure)

19.
(I tried to build a purple martin house
with many round doors
like an apartment complex
but none checked in
it fell apart as soon as one landed
I was a bad builder
their rich *tchew-wew* laughed at me

what made me think I could repair her mind)

20.
after a while all she wore was pajamas
scuffling across the floor in slippers

she did not know where she was
I'd answer
home

she'd ask
where's that

I'd respond
where the heart is

(momentary silence while she puzzled it out)

eventually I'd remind her
it's time for me to go

she would be curious and question
who are you

she was not being metaphysical

     21.
the quick wingbeats of a peregrine falcon
its *kek, kek, kek*

     22.
so I left her
I visited less and less
I forgot to visit

months flocked away

black birds roosted in my heart
blackening out memory

and then
she was gone

     23.
she had died in her sleep

she simply slipped away
in a boat of silence

broken wings moving in pajamas
her voice circling
who are you

I do not have a good answer

Bored Inquiry

Wild imagination brings out the best in me
I contemplate series of twisted memory
Finding myself frustrated with anxiety
Disappointment repeats itself busy
I loose interest in the scenery

Every motion remains senselessly dreary
Laughing in misery
Tediously dull moments of greenery
Lack interest

My curiosity roams
With doubt I ask the question
What's it all about
Twisted turns of conversation
Uninterested talk
Dull

Unable to move I am forced to walk
Repetitive chores
Become a bore
Asking almost demanding
Requests that need not be ignored

I make my way through
Accepting
Difficult to endure
Inevitably similar
Definitely confused
Seeking information
Distracted
Personally Unaware

Simply I don't care
This is not me
I may never get out of here
Trapped inside
Everyday activities decline
You do not see me
Yet inside I cry

Andrena Zawinski

The Way It Is

She staunchly insists her single hospital bed
in the shared room with drawn blue curtain
is a wing of her private and sprawling apartment,
kindly offers to have lunch staff heat something up
at what she introduces as the spa she now owns.
She won't allow the television or music
that distract from her invisible manuscript.

She sits in dimming light in an eclipsing eve,
wanes small and thin. This is what it has become.

She vows, in yet another delusional bloom,
to incorporate tai chi into her yoga practice
while she is able only to stand then wobble
and drop into the wheelchair she is too weak
to roll. She demands her lipstick, the clothes
she squirreled away under the table ferreting
the latest escape route, then the passport

she needs to fly off in this phantasmagoria,
longing a gnawing hunger. This is the way it goes.

Under night's fading clouds, meteors shower
across stroked occipital and parietal lobes.
She wades through a trough of fog, confused
by the distance between herself and the world.
Jupiter kisses Juno. Venus births Cupid. Mars
is at odds with everyone, noisy, keeping her up
under the same sky that holds the rest of us

silent and still, eyes aflutter with spirits of dream
as we drift off into sleep. This is the way it is.

Dorothy Alexander

After the Diagnosis

He lasted another eight years, without pain
or discernible change. Just kept taking
the medicines. So many of them we had to make
a chart to trace the amounts and times
as he progressed through the day and the doses.

When his mind started going over the edge he
marked all the boxes at once and didn't remember
what he had taken, what he had not. Until near the end,
he would say to his children, "Is this the worst
Alzheimer's can do?" But, then that changed.

He lapsed into a teeth-grinding agony, floating
on a sea of pain, but stoic and stubborn like he was
in the old life, pulling out the needles, the tubing,
refusing to give in, eyes set in rebellion, glaring
in denial, chanting a death song (the same one we
had heard his mother sing) that faded in the waning
hours until it was only a faint whisper
that disappeared an hour before dawn.

Selections from the unfinished novel
Laugh As I Pass In Thunder

    Will looked at his grandmother, tilting his head slightly as if the angle of his vision would make clearer the depths of her memory, as if he could see into the space once inhabited by memory. He wondered when in the duration of time, each memory had faded to oblivion, or whether each memory existed eternally in a specific moment that his grandmother no longer had access to. Had she been exiled from eternity, from multiple and infinite eternities that may or may not one day be recovered in another form in another life? Was life itself a form of exile from which we retain certain memories while others fade as we glide unaware along the invisible road of duration?

"Why the hell are you looking at me like that?"

"Sorry," Will said as he sat up straight.

"Who are you?"

"I'm your grandson."

"I don't have a grandson. For God's sake, I'm not that old."

Will tilted his head again and looked into that space.

"That's not right, is it?"

"No," he said.

***

Will sat in the chair next to his grandmother's bed. She lay there with the mobile tray over her midsection and a crossword magazine open in front of her. Will stared at the dingy off-white walls.

"Are you comfortable?" he asked, picking up the controller for the bed. "Do you want me to raise it higher?"

"I don't know," she said. "Who cares. Stupid bed, anyway"

She seemed coherent. Not as distant as usual. She was ornery. Herself, they would say on days like this. Will wasn't sure what that meant. Wasn't sure how someone could not be themselves. She knew who he was today.

"Do you need help with the crossword?" he asked.

"Oh, this? I'm just writing any word that fits." She laughed.

He liked to hear her laugh. His childhood was filled with her laughter. She seemed more serious now when she wasn't herself. When she was a different self. When something seemed to be missing. Was it herself that was missing when she didn't laugh? Who did she become when she wasn't herself? Was it laughter that brought her back to herself? Or was seriousness the result of forgetting herself?

"Are you just going to sit there and not say anything?" she said.

"Sorry," Will said.

"What were you thinking about?"

"Nothing," he said.

"I was always afraid there was nothing going on in there," she

125

said. And she laughed again.

Will smirked.

***

Will sat next to his grandmother in the courtyard and watched the gardener pick out the dead flowers and weeds from the large flower bed in the center. She stared blankly across to the other end of the courtyard.

"Is that my brother Mike?"

"No, Grandma. That's just another man living here. He's not family. I don't know who that is."

"Well, who else would be living here but family? That's ridiculous. That must be Mike. Hmm, he's in a wheel chair, too. I guess we're all getting old."

Will didn't want to tell her that all of her brothers were dead. It didn't matter now.

Grief

It is so hard to grieve
Since the person you grieve
Stands before you
An empty shell of yesterday
Still loved
Still cared for
Still hoped after
But now a vacuum
Empty of intellectual processes
Super sensitive to emotions
Now internalizing profound feelings
Into catastrophic outbursts
That age and stress one's soul
Seeking supportive solutions to address the angst
And unravel the bursting emotions that transcend reality
With care and love

It's a Given

You take it for granted
    you might die in the dirt
    or be horribly wounded.
Of course you set it aside,
    hope your wife won't be a widow.
But you take it for granted
    you'll sleep in the rain, the cold,
    live with fear,
    watch your buddies disappear, one by one.
And in fifty years meet a guy
    from your old company and
    he doesn't remember you.
In fact he doesn't remember much
    of anything.
His wife smiles tiredly,
    doing her duty,
    taking it for granted—

(re)collection

identity is a collection of memories and perceptions
filled with gaps

every memory is a metaphor
of the past and present at the same time

every memory is an arrangement of shapes and colors
on a four dimensional surface

every perception is a knife that slices memory
into a thousand minuscule fragments

every perception is a needle and thread
that stitches memory back together

the same memory is different each time it is perceived

time is a ghost that haunts every memory and perception

dementia is a collection of memories and perceptions
wearing masks and haunting time

filled with gaps

"who is Frank Beaver?" my grandmother asks

"that's your husband," my brother says

"oh, that son of a bitch?"

Lights Out

In shallow water on the edge of a pond
the giant water bug stalks a leopard frog
latches onto it
with its proboscis injects digestive juices
sips the frog's liquified body as if with a straw.

My life is being
sucked away—

                                 boyhood on the farm

                Europe after the war

                                        the pyramids at Giza

                            words   *shotgun*

                                        glove

        garden rake

                                                newspaper

                              baseball

        football

                                      ice skates

                                            story-telling

                              playing jokes

                                                the way

home from church

who I am
—*left behind*
a rattling shell.

Bits of me that remain—

         half a grin

   joke without a punch-line

               too-tight bear hug
        moment of recognition

—*spark occasionally*
in the wreckage of my world.

They harbor no evil intent
neither bug nor disease
just go about their business of living
from the dying
no sadistic leer
no hard feelings
no feelings at all.

Now almost everything

       is gone

           my empty skin

   crumples

      nothing left inside

         will the last

   person out

       please

turn off the lights?

My Mother and I

"How come you're the boss now?"
"I just want to help you"
"But I'M the mother and YOU'RE 's!"
"I know, but you're having some problems with your memory"
"There's nothing wrong with my memory!
"I'm sorry, but there is"
"How dare you say that about your mother!"

I walk out of the living room,
Busy myself in the kitchen for a few minutes,
Go back into the living room
"Hi, mom! How are you doing?
"Great! What are we going to do today?

She loves going out
We go listen to a local Latin jazz group
I buy us each a drink
Before I know it, she's downed it all
She looks at my drink, which is still full
She's angry
"How come you have a drink and I don't?"

Sometimes I keep her busy with a book,
So I can get some things done,
She sits looking at it for quite a while,
I'm never sure whether she's really reading it,
She can still wash dishes if I set it up for her,
So I can keep her busy that way, too
I makes her feel good that she is helping out

Sometimes I try to get her to go to sleep before me.
So I can have a little time alone
At 10:00 I say, "Aren't you tired?

Don't you want to go to bed?"
"What do you mean? Aren't we going out tonight?
I'm already getting tired,
But I keep her up late playing cards and watching TV,
Maybe I can have a little time alone in the morning,
But when I get up at 7:00 she's already up
And needs some help getting dressed
She wants to know what's for breakfast.

We go shopping for Christmas
She loves to walk around stores looking at things
She picks out something she wants to buy,
A stuffed animal,
I put it in the cart,
Hide it when we get home,
Wrap it up for her Christmas present
She unwraps it with anticipation
"How did you know exactly what I wanted?"

I need to create as many of these happy moments as I can
Or else I would be crying all the time

My Mother Reads The Classics (I read to her)

Sestina by Elizabeth Bishop—even as a young woman I knew it was wrong the grandmother was sad and had to raise the child—the worst!
Fire & Ice by Robert Frost—a good poem, but I didn't like him. He was anti-Semitic?
Jabberwocky—does the younger generation still love it?
Rhyme of the Ancient Mariner—why is he telling that story? Why is he telling the wedding guest? Let's skip some.
The Owl and The Pussycat—the best.
Song by John Donne—something upset him a lot at the end.
Daffodils by William Wordsworth—Daff-o-dils!
Let me not to the marriage of true minds by William Shakespeare—aah!
Concord by Emerson—sounds like a classic.

Fear and Dementia

My aunt can't eat, think,
remember recipes,
how to start the oven,
turn off the burners,
brew coffee.

She gets lost
in the grocery store,
at her sister's house.
Forgets what year it is,
the names of her children.

Faces are unfamiliar.
Strangers take her
to see white coated men
who confuse her with questions.
She weeps, has no answers.

Sea Change

I
Recalling children's names became too hard,
although her eyes spoke when offered flowers;
familiar iris, roses, and clematis from the yard
still blooming from her old invested hours.

Once prized, her tools became forgotten
frets, like setting special forks for fish,
oysters, salad, dinner, ice cream, lemon,
the trident for grandmère's watermelon relish.

The pastry piping cones no longer make
the rippling buttercream bark for Bûche de Nöel,
fine blossoms, leaves, script for family birthday cake
with silver-beaded pistils for each petal.

Her thimble, needles, and pinking shears are gone;
the seam-matched jacket plaids long outworn,
beaded and embroidered dresses long outgrown,
kept with heirlooms for christening the newborn.

Books, piano too, are left behind.
Like lilies lie her potted paintbrushes, useless
for capturing still lifes. Captive, her divining mind
dowses television, hands no longer restless.

II
Darting about in her aquarium,
people, like schools of fish, tease the anemone
of ancient memory rooted in a passing medium.
Suddenly she smiles, amused—what was funny

in that moment? I cannot ask to fathom.
Would her lifeline grasp had been the kinder moral
than the slow exchange of mind, in ransom
to the creeping tangled plaque, for living coral.

We have survived that long, cruel journey,
the elder rage, the foggy fears of what comes next.
Smiling faces became the tender mercy
beyond the deconstruction of her text.

What are we to her now without the memories?
At first, startling apparitions; then company calling
with ephemeral hugs, new stories, and memes
from before the shipwreck she cannot recall.

Drowning in the cranial undertow,
she holds our hands that cling like blades of seaweed.
All we have we lose to Lethe when she lets go
without the history of our mutual need.

Kayak Dream

How do you describe a dream? They are disjointed and surreal. Not this one. It was tailor made for me. Yes, it was disjointed, but it made so much sense. See what you think.

Bob is fully tall and robust, dressed inappropriately in a light blue patterned pants and a long sleeve light blue shirt. The shirt and pants are a heavy coarse material. He is in a good mood, very light-hearted, talking with people, not interacting much with me. He's in and out of my sight.

There is a large body of water, a lake we have to cross in a kayak to get to the place where we are staying. I don't have a decent paddle and I've never paddled a kayak before. I also have a fear of deep, open water. Bob gave me a paper towel tube wrapped in foil to use for a paddle—someone gave it to him for me. Later in the dream I see the paper towel tube is now down to a nub and I don't know how that happened. How can I solve this problem of crossing the lake?

I have been depending on Bob to get a paddle and to get us home. He could always figure out an answer before. I feel my stomach pitch with this realization, now it's up to me. How else can we get home? Could we walk, drive? No, we don't have a vehicle and the lake is too big to walk around.

I can see women across the lake, they are lined up sitting on beach chairs and they are holding dustpans. I feel a surge of hope. This is my support group. They are one step ahead of me solving problems and they must have figured out a dustpan will work as a paddle. Improvise. I have to find a dustpan. The water is getting choppy and I know it will get worse later. We must cross soon. It is so frustrating and I am angry.

Bob and I walk into town looking for a place that might have a dustpan. We open a door at the end of a long building and there is a group of men having a meeting. They are joking and laughing and they ask us why we thought a drugstore was through that door. These are the neurologists. They see us once or twice a year. They don't have a dustpan and can't help me find one. They are busy and they need to go back to work.

There is another long building. The windows are papered over with larger-than-life-size sporting goods images. Maybe there will be a store inside where I can buy a real paddle. Inside the building a group of men is sitting on benches, waiting, alone. They are quiet, not speaking with one another. They are dressed for the outdoors in bulky jumpsuits in a shiny grey material. I know they have paid a lot of money for this adventure. My thought is, they won't like where they are going. In a small alcove there's a disposable thermos in a waste basket, maybe I can use this as a paddle. I am desperate to find something I can use. Outside a big grey bus is pulling out. I can't see through the bus windows, but I know the men are inside the bus now.

I feel panicky and trapped. Then I realize this is a dream. I have to get out of it, I have to pull myself out.

As I wake up, all the emotions I felt during the dream are still with me. My heart is pounding, my head is swirling with confusion, my stomach is clenched. At the same time I am aware this is a perfect description for what is happening to Bob and to me. It's almost humorous to see how perfectly the events match my life, how on one level it seems to make sense.

This much emotion does not go away immediately after waking. I carried the feelings of dread and confusion for several hours into the day. It was only after I was caught up in my daily activities I was able to shake it.

Weeks later, I can still recall that dream. I see my anger, my fear and my hopelessness wrapped up in the sequence of events. I also see I will keep going, keep trying to find answers, keep looking for a way to get us across the lake, with a paddle or a dustpan or a used thermos.

11-5-17

Joe Cowles & Jon @ Potrero.

Well, did we load the cooler?
John's going upstairs to lock
the doors! I'm sitting
for a minute in the sunshine.
We are about ready to go.
I think I have everything
packed to go, the clouds
are getting pretty cloudy
so we're going to leave.
Jon is turning off the water
and gas. Then we're about
ready to go. We've been
here a couple of days
and are ready to drive
home. John is going to go
empty the potty. We are
"about" ready to go! It is
8:51 on 11-4-17. Barometer
62% humidity.

Joseph Cowles

(written after his diagnoses)

141

Lennart Lundh

Up the Road from Weeki Wachee

My father cuts my mother's food.
She's as close to totally blind
as she can get without being.
They married in '46, in Sweden.
This is one way love works
in the apocalypse of aging,
of being unwarrantied owners
of imperfect, failing bodies.

A month from now, a feeble old man,
my mother-in-law's second husband,
will enter the dementia ward unaware.
They married in '58, in Chicago.
She is relieved, when memory permits,
to be relieved of caring for him.
She loves him like my father his wife.
This, too, is how it works near the end.

Mary McGinnis

Night Job

"Now I want to sleep:
I ask them for a clean towel a
good top sheet ...
how about a toilet that works,
that doesn't overflow, wetting the floor. I want the
jewelry back at the house, and my fuzzy
orange
blanket!
No one comes to help me shower. It's been two weeks!
I think my nephew, that
good for nothing,
took my favorite ring! His

job, he thinks, is to sell everything —
over my dead body, I told
Barbara and Penny.

Nights without sunsets:
I miss my patio;
got a patio I left behind.

How come I'm here?
tell me what happened. I

want to watch tennis, turn
on my tv —
better stop complaining; will try walking up and down the
hall until dark."

Shadowlands

Hummingbirds find her each year in my garden next to the Buddleia bush not far from the wild mint and oregano. Her ashes scattered over moist topsoil, an added nutrient to my yellow and red rose bushes that seem to thrive with her presence. Roses were her passion. Each summer I'd honor her in a cornucopia of color and aroma atop my kitchen table.

Her love of gardening became my passion as I grew older. She'd let me help her dig trenches around each rose bush, then scatter green pellets of rose food to encourage next year's growth. When the petals fell into the dirt, I'd collect them in a basket until there were enough to make rose perfume. Neighborhood children would come over to help me crush the rose petals

our cement driveway, then put them into small glass bottles filled with clear water while we'd add individual colors of crunched up crepe paper. Lined up on the sidewalk, the bottles reflected a rainbow of purples, reds, yellows, oranges. Other than the permanent stains on the driveway, we left no trace of those magical summers that soon turned into distant memories when she began to

live in the shadowlands. Pot roasts in pressure cookers with mashed potatoes and gravy turned into TV dinners. Morning routines of picking ripe peaches and apricots from our fruit trees turned into silences around the breakfast table. Years later when she moved into assisted living there was more silence; no laughing at my father's jokes, only blank stares into nothingness. An early riser, California's glorious sunlight would shepherd her outside to her garden, especially when the peach tree and avocado trees were bending with ripe fruit. We'd take plastic bowls to hold what the birds hadn't already attempted to eat. When she went into her shadowlands she seemed not to care about the harvest. She had a room on the second floor with a balcony that looked out on a flowering cherry tree. The fallen pink blossoms made a carpet of color along her wooden balcony and her hummingbird feeder, that she managed to keep filled with sugar water, attracted hummers all summer while she'd sit in her rocker looking out of the picture window. I bought a watercolor painting that a friend had done of pink cherry blossoms

that I keep on the wall of my bedroom in New Mexico, a reminder of when she lived in the light. Now, when I sit on the swing in my back patio I wait for a hummer to appear in my garden to remind me that she is still somewhere with the hummers and the roses basking in pure sunlight of eternity

Marmika Paskiewicz

A Poem for Trapped Things
(after John Weiners)

He used to talk about isohedra
or constellations
        Deneb   Altair   Vega
               Those stars. That dark night.
The way mountains looked to
ancient artists & philosophers
or how he missed Lake Michigan,
the Slovenian grandmother,
caramelized turnips.

He talked and watched in Ojo Feliz
        Canutillo
               Shadyside   wherever we were
Before.

Later,
        his mind betrayed
him,   his body made
awkward staccato motions
in sundown and sunrise.
He remembered one artist only—
Michelangelo.
        Hano Road unidentifiable—
the place he lived for thirty years—
        unidentifiable as Duxberry Avenue and
        my grandparents,
        the pavilion in Tesuque where
        he played banjo   danced   sang

Later,

in the wheelchair or
thrusting his
body from bed -
fighting with every muscle
the reptile consuming
him,   his mind

Later,
        in the living room
quietly he —
after not talking for days -
listening to… there was
always the music…
quietly he
said "Satie.
I've always
liked. That piece."

wings beating against the glass
no one will open

Megan Baldrige

Daughter's Poem of Regret, Mother's Day 2016

Dad died,
young sixty-something
suddenly.

Mom,
in love still
addressed, stamped
hundreds of envelopes,
letters
inside intoning,
"Thank you for your kind words",
Then sent the letters
to the attic.

She saved articles
about the funeral,
piled them
in attic trunks,
next to
Sunday crosswords,
half finished,
to be resumed
when she regained
her love of words.

Thirty years later
I curate the clutter,
clear her attic
of old papers
so she won't

burn up
in a housefire.

But she,
like the widows of India
had already burned
on the pyre,
when her
love died,
in 1985.

Forcing the Brother-in-law

Moved two cats, one fish, and the furniture
in a two-hour sweep
one month after the funeral,
caravan of trucks and a snowmobile trailer,
his siblings and hers
plus the grandchildren
hefting and slinging all he'd been hoarding,
food in the fridge, newspaper ads,
notes she made to keep him on track
when she couldn't get up. Sheets off the bed,
clothes on the hangers, chairs, table, lamp.

They've signed the paperwork
by Power of Attorney, rent paid
through the VA for assisted living,
his room set-up as if he were home.

Sister-in-law has adopted the cats,
his wife's final wish, and he now sits
in his favorite easy chair, watching the fish
turn graceful circles in its familiar
aquarium, confusion seeping across his face.

Standing

my father lies naked on the floor
I can't lift him   I call my brother
he can barely stand this   I consider the portals
we long to slip through

I cover my father with a blanket
this body of his once lifted whole roads
these soft fists once clenched and swung
and pounded

we try to help my father stand
my brother's feelings hover
like drone missiles wanting a target

years of shoving   shoveling
and evading took our father's strength

I want to stretch my legs into the sunset
my brother can barely stand this work

I pull underwear up our father's legs
ask him to lean one way   tell my brother
to pull the other side of the underwear

my brother can barely stand this
I call 911 to help us
raise our father

lift him   toss him in the air
put him to bed   spoon sweet food
in his mouth
we can't keep doing this
my brother says

November 30, 2015

Cup #1
Tune-Up Cafe
Waffles, decaf cafe au lait
White mug with two chips in the lip and a wooden stick stirrer.

On Saturday, I took my mother to lunch at the little deli on the senior "campus" where she lives. Her aide and I walked her over. I was nervous because she'd stumbled and fallen in the street the day before. It was my mother's 89th birthday. At the deli, she tried to order a "Rachel" sandwich. Rachel is the name of my sister who primarily cares for her—I was just visiting. There was no such item on the menu, but it wasn't totally crazy. I myself had a memory of such a special—maybe it was turkey.

This time, we both had egg salad. On the way back to her apartment, my mother was saying: I can do so many things myself! Look at all the things I can do. I can walk! I can eat. I can go to the deli all by myself!

In the elevator, she panicked and started crying. "I don't know which button to press," she whimpered. I hit number one. The elevator began to move. My mother started trying to hit all the buttons at once. I swatted her hand away.

"Our conversations are so awkward," she'd said earlier. "I talk naturally to other people but not to you. You don't tell me how you are. How are you? You need to ask ME questions. Ask me a question so I can answer."

June 11, 2016

Cup #36
Newbridge on the Charles
Dedham, Massachusetts, coffee from coffee pot

Me: would you like some more scrambled eggs?
My mother: no, thank you.
I sit down.
My mother: Before you sit down, I
want…gentlemen…GENTLEMEN!
Me: Excuse me?
My mother: I want GENTLEMEN!
She points.
Me: You want eggs?
My mother: yes

My mother: You wrote this book.
She points at *Seven Places In America*
Me: yes
My mother: It's great…great…and, just like you it is totally
RANDOM! I mean "seven" places, how random.
She laughs.

Incomprehensible story in fragments about a friend's children…went
to MIT…but they lost all his records…he said he wouldn't go to
college, he wouldn't go to a terrible college like UNIVERSITY OF
NEW MEXICO!

My mother: X. is devoted to her girls…her children. I just hope that
someday she can also fall in love and find a true love…get married.

Me: Mom, X. is married to Y., the father of her children.
She clutches her face in her hands: OH NO!

My mother: Why do you repeat everything I say?
Me: I'm trying to understand you
My mother: No one can understand me

Internal Intervention

You paint your toenails but stop at eight.
> It could be a fashion statement, dummy.

You interrupt in the middle of—
> I grow weary with what I am saying.

You have two different shoes on.
> They match my unmatched socks.

You left the stove on, idiot.
> I like my eggs hard.

You go from room to room and forget what—
> I've got a lot of things on my mind.

> I pity you.
> > I love you.

Takeover

I see you sitting in the clouds
smiling, your mind heavy
locked in the prison of dementia.

I am helpless and want to pull you out.
The law of noninterference will not allow it.
I waiver between anger and acceptance.

Brutally beating myself and letting go.
I drag through the five stages of death
and struggle to come to terms with the second

loss of you still to come when you leave the body
to step onto the rainbow bridge.
The first flood of tears left my body.

A second flood will come.
In the meantime, my mantra is live life
and love you in your present state.

Incoming

My mother is a sand castle,
dementia the tide,
merciless,
unrelenting,
wearing down the edges,
eroding the essential her-ness
that gave her shape—
memories, likes, dislikes,
grains of identity returning to the sea.
The tide takes her favorite color,
her love of fashion,
the Irish humor that bit hard,
the names of her children.

Joseph A. Farina

asymmetry

what worlds
do you wander
behind those eyes
that see
but do not recognize

am i there
in some small fashion
living in your present plane

do we share again our passion
do you know and call my name

we have become
joined separate vessels
keepers of each other's
dreams
unable to be shared
each in worlds
that parallel
unable to converge....

Gravity

I have watched
the white-braided woman
in the wheelchair
for half an hour.
    Her head ticks downward,
    slow as a minute hand,
    so sluggish, it rests
    at last on the table
    without impact.
        I saw the attendant
        park her there,
        pull from a bin labeled *Activities*
        an assortment of plastic blocks
        in bright colors,
        place her mottled hands
        on the blocks as if she were
        a child learning shapes and colors.
            The hands slumped
            off the table
            once the attendant disappeared,
            and the glacial slippage
            of the head began,
                quiet as time in this place
                where people go wordlessly,
                where no one hears
                flesh meet wood
                or registers the difference.

Caryl McHarney

161

Gracie Panousis

I Undress my Mother

And she does not try to cover herself.
she does not look away from my eyes.
she stares right at me
and, with recognition,
her face splits into a soft smile.

We sidle into the shower together
an oyster and its pearl
I wear a bathing suit.
unlike my mother
I still feel shame in my nakedness

Her skin is loose and thin
as delicate as an orchid's petals
the breasts that sustained my life
are flat and empty
her torso narrow
the hair on her body sparse

I work the shampoo into her pink scalp
Umm — smells like cookies
she murmurs
as the vanilla scent fills the stall

Remember how I hated having my hair washed?
I ask her
Me and Daddy had to chase you all over the house
She chuckles

then shyly,
I like this

We step out onto the peach ceramic tile
and I envelop her in a white robe
I tie the belt around her waist
but I do not let her go

Startled only briefly
she hugs back in return
giving me her whole weight
leaning into my arms

"There But For . . ."

First light shoots a searing quill
shocking me into immediate consciousness,
quickly followed by the momentary,
alarming, disorientation
that occurs when waking in a strange place.

Almost immediately,
confusion yields to comprehension
and ricocheting heart rhythms abate.
serotonin suffuses mind and body

But in those brief seconds
of bewilderment
my self connects soundly
with my mother's progressing
Senility.

Marilyn C. O'Leary

How to Lose a Spouse

My friend's wife—early onset Alzheimer's.
He kept her home as long as he could
and put her in care after vowing
he never would.
He went to see her every day.
When she didn't recognize him anymore
he got a girlfriend.
He still went to see her every day.

My sister-in-law has moved her husband
into a "memory" facility, so-named
because its patients have none.
She visits every day, trying to help him find
something to do, but she can't, because he can't.
He doesn't enjoy her guitar playing
or poetry reading.
When she is not visiting him
she fills her days with classes
and tries not to feel free.

My neighbor's husband has
a particular kind of Alzheimer's.
She studies up on it
and tries to anticipate each step.
She methodically takes over
the bookkeeping, investments,
insurance, household maintenance.
But she didn't anticipate the accident.
She now does all the driving.

and still tries to plan for the next step,
but isn't sure what   it   will   be.

Another friend's husband has Alzheimer's, too.
She meditates, paints, does yoga
loves him, gets upset, gets help,
stays in the present, goes to the future,
cries, and doesn't know what else to do.

The Parting

Intently one eye watched me,
She always wanted to be near me,
She loved me unconditionally,
But I didn't want her here,
Why God, this way, why?
But I knew, she had always wanted to be near me,
Until the end was near,
Until I had to say the words,
Grandma is waiting for you on the other side,
My heart was breaking,
She always wanted to be near me.
I had to let her go,
I cried out Mom,
And she let me close her eye.

Dementia

Senility possesses my aunt,
creates an anxious, confused stranger.
Disconnected crazy
combined with paranoia
constantly spills from her mouth.

She smiles when I visit,
seems to recognize
family but cannot remember
my name or exactly
how we're related.

Some days she is content
living at the care facility,
welcomes company,
emerges for meals,
music or parties.

Other times,
she claws at windows,
cries she doesn't belong here,
just wants to go home, return to
familiar kitchen and garden.

The evening protocol

As the sun goes down,
I stand between the fading light
and the darker dark,

trying to keep the fangs at the door
from entering our waking hours,
his dreams at night.

We watch *Everybody Loves Raymond*,
and he laughs and laughs,
and I laugh with him.

He may or may not follow
Jeopardy, and what comes next
forgotten every day,

something I put him through:
the drops in the green bottle,
the pills—two sizes and shades of pink,

the orange and turquoise capsule.
I tuck him in, and give him a peck,
or he blows me a kiss,

on faith, who knows who I am,
friend, caregiver, the woman
who's boss here. Whatever *here*
is. Not home, never home.

New Moon

Your sliver of silver yesternight
melts today into moon that's now
hidden from probers of memory
but not from inner eyes of one
known as soulsearcher or lover
finding light from a bolder fire.

You Left the Refrigerator Open

That's how I knew. You didn't notice your hair jutting out sideways or half your mouth dragging down when you tried to talk.

You would not let me call the hospital or your doctor, so I sprinted upstairs, found your brown metal phone book but couldn't remember your doctor's last name. I thumbed through the whole thing and somehow found it anyway.

In the kitchen, you watched me slow-motion dial the yellow rotary phone.

"Call an ambulance. Don't wait," the receptionist said.

The paramedics took you away. You probably don't remember any of this.

Later, I brought my dog to the rehab, and you fed her your hospital Hoodsie. We watched *Seinfeld* every night. You half smiled as you told me your hospital neighbor liked it when I wore shorts.

In a month, you came home. I know you remember that. You could not swallow solids, but you were home.

The next stroke blacked out half your brain. That's what your doctor told us. Even so, when he asked how you were, you said, "Fine."

170

That first night of your second stroke, I sat up with you to watch the Red Sox. Your machines beeped as I narrated. I told you Manny was just walking to a ball that dribbled out to left. You laughed past the frozen side of your mouth. "He always does that," you said.

Your night nurse fell in love with you in less than a day. She cried when she hugged you goodbye. You might remember that.

Then it was hospital, rehab, hospital, rehab, hospital, nursing home. And you never came home. C Diff, pneumonia, C Diff, pneumonia, swallow test upon swallow test upon swallow test. And you never came home.

You could no longer see but saw movies in your mind. You won't remember them as anything but real. You seemed to be dreaming all the time and told me about the two blonde nurses who were sisters. They bathed you. I liked when you told me that dream and wished for my own blonde nurses.

Afternoons, I sometimes left work early to wheel you around outside the brick building. "When I say 'I love you,' I mean it," you said, your harsh voice letting me know I was in trouble for not remembering.

On the rare Friday night, I brought beer to your room. We watched *Seinfeld* or the Sox. You still remembered every player and what team he'd been traded from, yet you couldn't drink even a sip of water past your feeding tube. My dog licked the drips from your machine, like it was chocolate milk you poured out just for her. Broken blood vessels rouged your shadowy cheeks, as though you

171

were healthy still. That Christmas, we gave wine and cards to every nurse.

As many times as you asked, I refused to toilet you. Had you been well, you never would have wanted your daughter seeing you that way. Every four minutes, you asked me to find someone to bring you to the bathroom. I hope you don't remember feces gunked under your nails when the staff didn't clean you right. Those dark crescent fingernails, the smell I'd like to forget.

The last January, the last swallow tests, the last procedure, the last days, last hours in the snow-bright room, we sang to you past your morphine, tried to sing you out of your fear. "I will bear you up, on eagles' wings," we sang, your favorite song, your tenor voice behind ours, somewhere.

I told your nurse I wanted a few drops of morphine to go. She didn't laugh. You would have laughed had you been awake. At your wake, we dressed you in your favorite St. Patrick's Day sport coat, kelly green to match the shamrocks on your tie. You won't remember that.

Your memory has pushed into mine now. I go to your childhood home and remember the seven-year-old you, punching your sister in the arm after the scarlet fever shots. I remember how much you hated the quarantine, how you longed to be outdoors.

I remember the Flood of '27, when you were just four and so euphoric after the river swept the outhouse away. Six months later, you returned home to calcified silt blanketing the basement. Standing over the kitchen sink, you and Gramma hand scrubbed each piece of

172

coal. You heard your mother swear for the first and only time of your life. "It's all right, Mum," you cooed.

I remember it all for you.

Dementia

A story of love, hate, and forgiveness. She was as a child in her conversation. Her selected memories spilled out amid childhood games in her old neighborhood street. She frequently desired to be taken back home where she had been free amid her friends. She did not remember me, so it seemed, until she muttered under her breath, "She never believed I would take her away." I wonder what she meant. Was she speaking of me? Then I understood, she was speaking of my mother whom she took me from. She had told me she, mother, had given me away. Now I knew the truth. Between her thoughts of the past, I was still. The one who betrayed her love and chose to leave when my father left. She tried to hurt me in many ways and I had resentment in my heart that would not let me forgive. I saw something then, that sparkle of childhood and times past that overcame her mind. She no longer recognized her own time. Her children were lost to her. In her mind, she was still nine. I could not help but forgive the damage she had done, the hatred I once felt, her rejection and her spite. God had forgiven her, why not I? The word mom which I could no longer say to her and at a loss for a better word, I had replaced with a term of endearment of her name.

Janet Simon

Displaced OLDCART

Knock on treatment room door
Interrupts quiet conversation
Between handholding couple
Exchange greetings
Chat about the hot weather
Proceed with intake where ventriloquy occurs
Onset
        Location
        Duration
        Characteristics
        Aggravating factors
        Relieving factors
        Treatment so far
The voice of my patient emanates from another
Mind split off from physical body

Empty Bark

Lonely tall Pine
your gutted stump
stands there
a Cascara*
heart torn out
by fire and ice
a thousand insects
gnawing your foundation
yet
your essence gone
you still cling tenaciously
by strong roots
reluctant to leave
the pristine wilderness
of Yosemite

Emptiness entered your center core
scoped out your entrañas**
just as Alzheimer disease
steals away
a person's nucleus
taking with it
the mind
leaving only a shell
in place.

Would that I could wrap
my arms
around your invisible center

make you whole
bring back the beauty
that was you
rather than
your lost interior
so
you could thrive
once again
as
a flourishing Pine
on the road to Bridal Fall

*Cascara; bark of tree, hull
**Entranas; entrails, the internal parts of anything

Jennifer Maloney

A Dog in the Afternoon

—inspired by Ann Maloney, Barbara Sweeny and Ann Turner
Kessemeier, who asked the question.

Is there a dog in the afternoon?

Yes, Mom.

And there are eggs and coffee
in the morning. There is a warm bath tonight,
and a terry cloth robe
the color of the black-capped chickadees
playing in the shaggy spruce in our front yard
and slippers
lined with fleece. There are small pills,
yellow, blue, and a sofa
with a marmalade cat you like to talk to,
and that likes to talk to you.

There are also, always,
my hands to hold. My voice that sings with yours,
"Irish Eyes" and "I'll take you Home Again,
Kathleen," and "Mick McGilligan's Ball." My arms
that curl around your shoulders
when you'll let them. When you're not
too angry, or afraid. That's the dog,

the black dog that comes in the afternoon.
Sometimes he growls, snarls. Sometimes he just cries.
But we know him now,
you and I. We know him, so

we don't have to be afraid.
We can pet him. Stroke his head. We can
help him
to remember
if not our names, our faces,
then at least our hands
and arms. Maybe the scent
of coffee and eggs
in the morning. Maybe
the warmth of a cup of tea.
Maybe a biscuit
for the dog in the afternoon.

Remember the One Who Remembers You Not

A single tear ran down her cheek
one of many from her ducts
heart so heavy, sodden with grief
body grown weary, hope all spent.

She came to visit her loving Mom
a regular routine, thrice each week
she'd brush Mom's hair, put on warm socks
answer the same question dozens of times.

Mom talked much about daughter Claire
how kind and caring, so full of grace
hoping she'd pay an occasional visit—
"I am that Claire she speaks of fondly.

Damn this plague which robbed her mind
of happy thoughts, of love we cherished
leaving behind an empty shell
void of times most happily shared.

Don't think me cruel or light of spirit
I love my Mom with all my heart
it grieves me deeply to see her so
to realize she will never return.

May God take her to her just rewards
and clear this fog which engulfs her so
free me from my guilt and daily anguish
who will help me when my memories lapse?"

Marmika Paskiewicz

What Are the Odds?

—

Growing older—
how memory deceives us
how we joke—
a senior moment
ha ha
how someone says—
"You've lost so much memory!"
unthinking   unkind
perhaps meaning to be kind
but wanting to say, needing to say
            she won't admit it
How we think if we notice it
            chase it
            take a pill
            walk 30 minutes
            do a crossword puzzle
            if we admit it
                        like a 12-step program

that   we   can
                        control this galloping horse
this ferocious wind
            that jumps fences without a saddle or bridle.

Kathy Lundy Derengowski

Butterflies and Moths

My mother had Alzheimer's
Where was the poetry in that
No rhythm, no reason, and no rhyme,
No cadence, only chaos.
No song, only sorrow.

The first signs
A mind adrift,
An almost charming scatteredness
Butterfly thoughts
Fluttering away,
As she chased them, and then
...forgot to chase them.

Then, not so benign
Mind moths
Ravenous and cruel,
And no way to re-weave
The tattered textile of her mind

And finally, for her,
No sad remembering
And no regrets
Neither worry, nor anxious fear
—Not knowing, what she no longer knew
She had already left of course,
It was so sad to watch.
There was no poetry in that.
But poetry was all we had, for help.

Karen Downs-Barton

A Walk in the Park

A name on a plaque on a bench in the park
I stop his hand from picking the flowers
beguiled by leaves and wrappers in windblown dance
a park trip in his favourite pyjamas

I stop his hand from picking the flowers
touching a nerve I'd switched off in my head

the park trip in his favourite pyjamas
"And can we go home to my real home instead?"

Touching a nerve long switched off in his head
he hums a calypso, so clear in his memory

and 'can we go home to my real home instead?'
'Tomorrow', I'll say, then 'Tomorrow' again.

I hum a calypso, so clear in my memory
consoled by leaves and wrappers in windblown dance
tomorrow I'll lay, then tomorrow again,
flowers by a plaque on a bench in the park.

Wedding Bells

When she looks out at the Qutab Minar, in Delhi, misted browns and grays settle into a bright red triangle, the tallest minaret she remembers someone saying, now turned into one large red brick, gold rays soaring into space.

She regards Howard carefully. He tells her time and time again that she's wrong about this, wrong about that to the point she is afraid to say anything. "Have we seen the Georgia Embassy yet, Howard?" Her voice tremors. Yet he has the kind of eyes she thinks of as manly, with a set of endearing crow's feet. He stands at a distance, this man, who is called Howard, smells familiar, and she tries hard to place him in her past, the effort making her sleepy. She must lie down and spreads her shawl closer to the one-hundredth spiritual UNESCO sites they have visited in the last few weeks.

Her toes tingle, and her hands rise to shade her eyes from light, and she feels a migraine from hell descending into her head. If only she can find a cold glass of water. After she rings the hospital bell, she's sure she hears a *drilbu*. Oh, dear, is that Hindu or Buddhist? She won't dare ask Howard. What beautiful bells!

The nurse wipes Rosemarie's brow, so gently, so kindly, and Rosemarie smiles, even as her own name escapes her.

So much sheer material. So much glitter. She's at the wedding now, and most things are blurry. Why is the bride waiting for the groom? Isn't it usually the bride entering the room, the groom waiting next to his best man? Rosemarie remembers slightly the smiles of her own mother and father at their wedding, yes, she's quite sure she married a smart young man, she is sure his name is Jessie.

More tinkling of bells nearby, tingling of toes at a distant.

The nurse explains to Howard as if he is the one who has dementia, "Your wife's body is disassociating from her mind now. That is not something uncommon. People walk all over looking for something they may have lost twenty years ago."

Howard rubs and then slaps his hands together as if that may be a common way he dismisses people, and then says, "Rosemarie's body is wilting along with her mind." A bedpan rattles, and he disappears.

Rosemarie is no longer trying to get Howard's attention at the dance. The groom has ridden into the large barn, outlandish, she thinks, on a white mare, a *ghodi*, embellished in decorations, predominantly yellow and red. More red like the minaret, more red like her silk dress. She may even dance. She will never leave the party before its end. As long as the garland of flowers, the jasmine *gajra*, scents the home where she resides, and the sweet odor intensifies as a paean to the love between bride and groom, man and woman, Rosemarie stays.

185

Almost Dinnertime

The woman in the blackandwhite circletop approaches,
a tin necklace with round discs hanging low from her neck.

"Four quadrants," she reports. Agitated.
"We need to tell someone now!"
The goat and chickens glide across the window,
but still she continues.
"It's the transformative transfornascent junction!"
I don't like her to talk to me.

In her bright redblouse, Joan listens,
then tells us he grabbed her arm,
evenafter she told him not to.
 "It hurt." The whisper hides her tears.
Joan's long gray hair falls and quietness surrounds us.
The greenworkers busily walk in crisscross lines.

I know who the man is.
He's the swollen rubberman who grabs my shoulders.
I try to stay away from him,
but the halls are dark
and he fidgets around the corners.
When I hurry to find my way out,
he's always there, bouncing sideways.

The goat and chickens are slow now.
The goat stretches and the chickens nod their heads.

As we shuffle toward the longtables in the big room,
a loudwoman over there crytalks to a greenworker
who hummms back

186

after eachofherbursts.
I don't want to hear,
but the woman crytalks louder and louder.
Joan looks up.
She says the loudwoman is trying to explain, to get an answer.

The old manwoman sitting at the end of table six reads a thick book.
It's almost dinnertime.

Michael after Midnight

"Come in, Michael, come in,
your underwear are wet,
there are scratches on
your legs. Are you cold?
Sit down, I'll take care of you.
It's okay, you're okay."

"You're always welcome,
any time, day or night.
That's what friends are for.
Not sure what to do? I'll
put on your movie."

The Sandpiper runs
once more as 1974
lights dim confusion,
empty rooms for a moment illuminated.

The gift of naming is granted
Michael's mind wraiths. "Yes,
Elizabeth Taylor is picnicking with
Richard on a plaid blanket at
Carmel Beach where we
dug for pirate treasure.
It's too dark to go dig
out there right now, Michael."

"Oh look, she caught the bird,
the little sandpiper,
but his wing is broken.

He will get better.
Liz is taking good care
and he'll fly again."

Monterey pines shushing sound
in the late night; on the beach,
the tide is going out
in Carmel-by-the-Sea.
Michael soothes into
sofa sleep. Always friends,
now watcher and watched,
this sandpiper cannot heal.
"It's okay, Michael, it's okay."

(Hush a bye)

It takes more than one shake
of her shoulder to wake her,

(Don't you cry)

so deeply asleep, her body curled
between the rails, head pushed
into pillow. I sing and
stroke her forehead
the way she used to stroke mine, seducing me,

(Go to sleep, little baby)

seducing me into unwanted naps when I was four.
Finally, they open and I
look into the sage green eyes of a
drowned child, fathoms deep, with
no desire to rise.
Still, she smiles a bit
at me and my little dog,

(When you wake, you shall have)

makes reassuring noises and
sinks again.

(All the pretty little horses)

I anoint her with my tears and
my little dog's kisses.
She is dying.

(Blacks and bays)

She has been dying for a long time,
practicing for it in her sleep,
her whole life, really.

(Dapples and greys)
And, I realize now,

(All the pretty little horses)
I have too.

Carol Moscrip

Ashes

what a great place to be buried, near the Golden Gate
scattered in a thoroughfare to and from the Pacific,
my mother never sought peace and quiet, always preferred a party,
she had prearranged and prepaid for this one,
I wish now we'd had a solitary trumpeter on board
to baffle the rhythm of the waves, to sing the single note of grief,
as I read a list of sentiments compiled by my sister
adding how Mother had loved red, her college color,
her ashes transported to the center of the bay in the Neptune,
she would have adored the pagan name, ever an agnostic
until she had almost reached the end of her mind,
then a fierce atheist with a faith as sudden
and ardent as a belief in Christ's face
on a piece of French toast, how she hated churches,
"I know there isn't anything after,
I just know it," with fervor she announced
to me shortly before she left us just her body
slumped back in a wheelchair with vacant eyes,
she would have died had she known,
a mere lump to transport and feed and wipe,
she didn't have to go to such lengths
just to demonstrate there is no God,
we prayed a godless prayer for her
that she didn't sense a thing,
we mourned her breathing absence nearly four years
until her lungs had no energy to rise and fall,
at last her ashes scattered into the bay of the city
where she was born, San Francisco,
the only city with class was another of her devout beliefs
did I mention the little waves that offered themselves up

192

over and over to bury the dark mass of her body
and lap it up they did, to the last bit of ash she merged
with the currents as the boat rocked us
my sister and I nervously shaking any dust from the metal box
down to the last particles that clung to the sides

Previously Published

"Missing Persons" by Scott Wiggerman was previously published in the anthology *Forgetting Home* (Barefoot Muse, 2013).

"Ashes" by Carol Moscrip in *San Diego Poetry Annual* in 2016.

All poems by Shirley Blackwell were previously published in her book, *Already There*.

Daniel McGinn's poem, "Note To Self" was previously published in an anthology entitled *Incandescent Mind* also All three of the poems submitted were previously published in *The Moon, My Lover, My Mother & The Dog*, my full-length book of poetry that was published in March of this year by Moon Tide Press. An early version of the poem "Mother Losing Her Mind" was published by Bank Heavy Press.

Gayle Lauradunn's poem "Grandfather" appeared in her book, *Reaching for Air.*

Sally Kimball's "The Parting" was published in the 2016 Las Positas College Anthology *SPARKS*.

Georgia Santa-Maria's poem "Puzzle Pieces" appeared in her book *Lichen Kisses*

"I Undress my Mother" by Conway Panousis Published in *Toward Forgiveness, An Anthology of Poems*, edited by Gayl Teller.

Previously published by Lennart Lundh: "Up the Road from Weeki Wachee:" *Memory Care* (Beautiful Blasphemy, 2018) "The Value of Knowledge:" Illinois State Poetry Society (Web site, 2017) "Another Time, Another Country:" *Poems Against Cancer 2018* (self-published fundraiser for the St. Baldrick's Foundation, 2018)

Rich Bouchier's poem "Whenever I Get An Idea, A Light Bulb Full of Gunpowder Appears Above My Head" first appeared in the April 2018 edition of the online literary journal *Runcible Spoon*.

Suzanne Niedzielska's poem was previously published in her chapbook, *Black Tie & Tales,* with a limited circulation (2007, Shadow Poetry).

Kathy Lundy Derengowski's poem "Butterflies and Moths" was previously published in the anthology of the Lake San Marcos Writers

Lauren Camp's poem "Is Empty he Says" was previously published in *Ducts*. The poem "Memento Mori" was first published in *Belmont Story Review*, and "Five Days of a Day and a Night" was published in *december*.

"Sixty" by Mary Dudley was first published in *Quintet*, (2013) *Watermelon Press* and in *Value* (2017) Beatlick Press.

"Take" by Rina Ferrarell first Appeared in *VIA* (*Voices in Italian Americana*), "The Evening Protocol" first appeared in *Paterson Literary Review* and "Second Wife" was first published in *5AM*.

"Dementia" by Wendy Rainey previously appeared in *Chiron Review*.

'The Queen is Dead' by Juleigh Howard-Hobsonhas appeared in *Our Otherworld* (Red Salon Press),

Andi Penner's poems "Dostoyevsky and Pajamas" and "Her Chimayo Jacket" were previously published in *Rabbit Sun, Lotus Moon*. *Mercury Heartlink*,2017.

"Terra Incognita" by Linda Flaherty Haltmaier was a finalist for the 2018 Robert Frost Poetry Prize and appears in her new book, *To the Left of the Sun* and "The Upside of Dementia" appears in her collection, *Rolling up the Sky*.

"After the Diagnosis" first appeared in *Borrowed Dust: Poems & Other Parables,* by Dorothy Alexander (Village Books Press, 2006) "Sibyl's Question" and "What We Don't Talk About" (under title, "Taking Care") both appeared first in *Blood and Thunder: Musings on the Art of Medicine*, University of Oklahoma School of Medicine, Issue 8, Fall 2008.

Richard Vargas poem was in his book *Guernica, revisited* press 53, 2014.

Contributor Biographies

Dorothy Alexander (6, 64, 123) is the author of five poetry collections, two multi-genre memoirs, and two volumes of oral history; a founder and curator of poetry for the Woody Guthrie Folk Festival in Okemah, Oklahoma; as well as a lawyer and municipal judge. She was the 2013 recipient of the Carlile Award for Distinguished Service to the Oklahoma Literary Community from the Oklahoma Center for the Book.

Megan Baldrige (148) is an Albuquerque poet who is trying to write about the art, politics and community of knitting, hoping that the writing and the knitting will help her keep all her strands as knit together as they have ever been.

Shirley Blackwell (62, 72, 92) of Los Lunas has published two poetry books that were finalists in the NM-AZ Book Awards. She has served on the Boards of the NM State Poetry Society since 2008 and of its parent organization since 2014 as chair of the national NFSPS College Undergraduate Poetry competition. She was chair of the NFSPS College competition during 2014-18, and have been NFSPS 1st vice chancellor since June 2018.

Joanne S. Bodin, Ph.D., (144) is an award-winning author and poet. Her book of poetry *Piggybacked*, was a finalist in the New Mexico Book Awards. Her novel *Walking Fish,* won the NM Book Award and the International Book Award in gay/lesbian fiction. *Orchid of the Night*, was a finalist for the Eric Hoffer Award and the NM Press Women Communication Award, and won the NM Book Award in LGBT fiction. **www.joannebodin.com**

Rich Boucher (8) lives in Albuquerque and his poems have appeared in *Cultural Weekly, Tinderbox Poetry Journal, Soft Cartel, Philosophical Idiot, MoonPark Review* and *Menacing Hedge,* among others, and he has work forthcoming in *Street Poet Review.* Hear more of his work at richboucher.bandcamp.com. He loves his life with his love Leann.

Lauren Camp (16, 61, 76) is the author of four books, most recently *Turquoise Door.* She is the recipient of the Dorset Prize and a Black Earth Institute fellowship. In 2018, she presented her dementia poems at the original Mayo Clinic and the Alzheimer's Association New Mexico Caregiver Conference. www.laurencamp.com

Gregory L. Candela (24) has resided in New Mexico since 1972. He has scholarly articles in American and African American literature, a volume of poetry (*Surfing New Mexico,*) has written seven produced plays, and edited 6 volumes of poetry and prose. More recent publications include poems in many publications. A member of the New Mexico State Poetry Society, he served on the Selection Committee for Albuquerque's first Poet Laureate and serves as a Poet in the Classroom. His Poem "Cementerios de Nuevo Mexcio" was nominated for a 2018 Pushcart Prize, and his second collection of poetry, *Shallow-Rooted Heart* is newly published by Dos Gatos Press.

Dr. Maria Chavez (127, 176) holds a BS, MA and Ed.D from UNM. She founded UNM Family Development Program in 1985. The White house honored program as one of three best early childhood programs in the USA in 1993. She aided mother, mother in law and retired to care for her Alzheimer husband.

Gracie Conway Panousis (108, 110, 162) is an Ohio native who feels a deep affinity and great respect for the hard-working, kind people of her home state. She currently lives and works on Long Island in New York. Her essays and poetry have been published in *The New York Times*, *The English Journal* and *Toward Forgiveness, An Anthology of Poems*.

Star Coulbrooke, (46, 150) Poet Laureate of Logan City, Utah, and Utah State University Writing Center Director, is co-founder and coordinator of Helicon West, a bi-monthly open readings/featured readers series. Published widely in lit mags and anthologies, Star's poems are also available in chapbooks, notably *Walking the Bear,* which can be accessed through the Digital Stacks at the University of Utah Marriott Library. She has published two poetry collections, *Thin Spines of Memory* and *Both Sides from the Middle.*

Barbora Cowles (138) has worked with her husband on their publishing venture, Event Horizon Press since 1990. She has been an educator and has worked in the corporate world as well. She prefers publishing.

David Lavar Coy (68) has degrees from the University of Wyoming and the University of Arkansas in literature and creative writing respectively. He is the author of three books of poems. His poems have appeared in *Antioch Review, Slant, CNR, Widener Review, gulfstreaming, Spoonriver, Poet Lore, Magma 34, Moon City Review, Poetry in Performance,* plus in the anthologies *Manifest West* and *La Llorona.*

Deborah Coy (99, 156) is an editor with award winning Beatlick Press. which has published about thirty books. Her work appears in many publications and online. She has three books available. Her book of poetry *Beyond the End of the Road* is available on Amazon as are her books for children.

Susy Crandall (51, 66, 190) writes poetry to save her own life. She has been published in the *Fixed and Free Anthology, Adobe Walls,* and *The Mas Tequila Review.*

Victoria Crawford (188) is a poet who has helped care for a parent and a neighbor living in dementia. She frequently writes about health issues, having published in journals such as *Hektoen International, Wraith Infirmities Muse, Pacific Poetry,* and *Cargo Literary.*

Casey Derengowski (180) has been writing for many years, professionally as a teacher, later as a probation officer and personally as a self-imposed hobby. He has been published in *Summation, Chicago Poetry Press* and *Silver Birch Press* as well as various other anthologies.

Karen Downs-Barton (55, 86, 183) is a neurodiverse poet studying History of Art with Creative Writing BA. Based close to Stonehenge her quarryman's cottage is held together with mud and hair mortar. Her non-poetic occupations include magician's assistant and dance teacher (Middle Eastern and tango). She is published by *Abyss, Word Gathering, The Curly Mind, The Fem Lit'* and *Otoliths* amongst others.

With an M.A. in American poetry, **Mary Dudley** (18, 26) earned a Ph.D. in early child development. She's written about and worked with young children, their families, and teachers. She's published three chapbooks of poetry and her poems have appeared in a number of collections, including *La Llorona; Sin Fronteras, Zingara Poetry Review; Value; Poets Speak anthology;* and *Weaving the Terrain.*

Janet Eigner's (48, 60, 87) *What Lasts is the Breath (2013)* a Winner in the AZ-NM Book Awards 2013, a Finalist in the NM Newspaper Women Contest, 2015, Puddinghouse chapbook: *Cornstalk Mother (2009),* a Poetry Foundation Poet, on *American Life in Poetry,* dance articles. Forthcoming, a collection *12 backpack trips, 4 decades into Grand Canyon,* a labyrinth of emotional safety, cosmology, geology and spirit, in the lap of Mother Nature, both concrete and metaphoric.

Joseph A. Farina (159) is a retired lawyer in Sarnia, Ontario, Canada. Several of his poems have been published in *Quills Canadian Poetry Magazine, Ascent* and in *The Tower Poetry Magazine, Inscribed, The Windsor Review, Boxcar Poetry Revue,* and appears in the anthology *Sweet Lemons: Writings with a Sicilian Accent.* He has had poems published in the *U.S.A* magazines *Mobius, Pyramid Arts, Arabesques , Fiele-Festa* and *Memoir(and)* as well as in *Silver Birch Press "Me, at Seventeen" Series.* He has had two books of poetry published — *The Cancer Chronicles* and *The Ghosts of Water Street.*

Jeanne M. Favret (22, 106) is a member of the New Mexico Poetry Alliance. She enjoys hearing contemporary poets read aloud, and she is fond of haiku. Her work has been published in *Turtle Music, Adobe Walls, Along the Rio Grande, Muse with Blue Apples, Medical Muse,* and *Weaving the Terrain.*

An immigrant from Italy, **Rina Ferrarelli** (36, 75, 168) has written many poems on subjects having to do with emigration, and has also translated the work of Italian poets into English. Her most recent collections are *The Bread We Ate* (Guernica), poetry, and *Winter Fragments* (Chelsea), translation. *The Winter Without Spring,* a book of poems from the viewpoint of a caregiver, is forthcoming from Main Street Rag in the fall.

Linda Flaherty Haltmaier (38, 54, 158) is an award-winning author and the Poet Laureate of Andover, Massachusetts. She is the winner of the Homebound Publications Poetry Prize for her collection, *Rolling up the Sky* (2016). *To the Left of the Sun* (Homebound Publications), was awarded the 2018 International Book Award for Poetry. Her work earned first place in the Palm Beach Poetry Festival Competition, finalist honors for the Princemere Poetry Prize and the Tucson Festival of the Book Literary Award, and been shortlisted for the Robert Frost Poetry Prize. Her poetry has appeared in *Ink & Letters, The Wild Word, Switchgrass Review,* and more.

Teresa E. Gallion (84, 157) is on a spiritual journey traveling and hiking mountain and desert landscapes. She has published three books: *Walking Sacred Ground, Contemplation in the High Desert* and *Chasing Light,* a finalist in the 2013 New Mexico/Arizona Book Awards. Her work has appeared in numerous journals and anthologies. You may preview her work at http://teresagallion.yolasite.com/

Iris Gersh (184) grew up in the Shawangunks and has lived in Albuquerque since '05. Her writing has been published in several literary magazines, including the 2017 *The Packinghouse Review*. She is Vice President of New Mexico State Poetry Society's board. She is working on a collection of poetry and a memoir about living in Greece.

Thelma Giomi, Ph.D. (7) is a clinical psychologist, published author and award winning poet. She is also someone who lives with a chronic (incurable) illness, Systemic Lupus. From the very essence of her being she draws from the challenges of coping with the necessity to cope and finds the invincible vitality within, a creative energy and passion for life. In her writing and public speaking she shares her experiences with chronic illness, aging and resilience. Her poems are joyful, encouraging and without apology, passionate.

Curtis Hayes (104) has worked in sawmills, greasy spoons, and as a grip, gaffer, and set builder in film productions. He's been a truck driver, a boat rigger, a print journalist and a screenwriter. His poetry has been featured in *Chiron Review, Trailer Park Quarterly, Cultural Weekly* and other small presses.

John Hicks (11) is an emerging poet: has been published or accepted for publication by: *Glint, I-70 Review, First Literary Review — East, Panorama, Midnight Circus, Mojave River Review, Sky Island Journal,* and others. He completed an MFA in Creative Writing at the University of Nebraska — Omaha in 2016.

Steven Hendrix (34, 124, 129) has a BA in Comparative Literature and an MA in English from CSULB. He grew up in Southern California and now lives in San Francisco with his family. His work has appeared in *Chiron Review, Drunk Monkeys,* and *Cadence Collective* among others.

Juleigh Howard-Hobson's (34, 124, 129) poetry has appeared in *The Comstock Review, Anima, L'Éphémère, The Lyric, Weaving The Terrain* (Dos Gatos), *Poem Revised* (Marion Street*), The Nancy Drew Anthology* (Silver Birch), *The Literary Whip* (Zoetic Press podcast) and other venues. Nominations include "Best of the Net", The Pushcart Prize and The Rhysling Award. An English ex-pat, she now lives in the American Pacific Northwest, by a deep dark forest full of oak and ash.

Faith Kaltenbach (47) is semi-retired and lives in Rio Rancho with her daughter and four grandchildren. Her poems have been published in *Poets Speak:Walls, Weaving the Terrain, Duke City Fix, Fixed and Free Anthology 2018.*

Kathamann (12, 21, 96) is a returned Peace Corps Volunteer/Afghanistan and a retired registered nurse. She has been active in the Santa Fe arts community for 30 years exhibiting in juried, group and solo exhibits. (kathamann.com) Her poems have occasionally been published in local and regional anthologies.

Mary Ellen Kelly (27) writes poetry for adults and literature for young children. In her retirement from college teaching, she enjoys volunteering for nonprofit organizations in her community that support children's literacy, immigrants, and individuals affected by cancer. Along with writing, photography gives her great pleasure.

Sally Kimball's (166) stories have appeared in *CWC Literary Review; 2015 Anthology Voices of the Valley: Word for Word; 2016 Anthology Sparks; and 2017 Anthology, Beyond the Window.* She is a Ministerial Counselor and finds her inspirations through work in the ministry and years in law enforcement. She lives in Bernalillo, NM

Sreekanth Kopuri PhD, (78) is a Telugu-speaking Indian English poet from Machilipatnam, India. He is the recipient of Dr. JK International award in 2015 for his poetry. He has recited his poetry and presented research papers in Oxford, Banja Luka, Caen, Gdanski, Dusseldorf and Wilkes Universities. His poems have been published or forthcoming in *Ann Arbor Review, Scryptic Magazine, Five 2 One, Vayavya, Paragon Journal, Foliate Oak Review, Halcyon Days, Oddball, Forty Eight Review, McKinley Review, Ariel Chart, Poetcrit, Indian Periodical, Deccan Chronicle* and *A Flood of Contentment* and elsewhere. Kopuri presently lives with his mother in Machilipatnam.

Jennifer Lagier (97, 135, 167) has published fourteen books, co-edits the *Homestead Review,* helps coordinate Monterey Bay Poetry Consortium readings. Newest books: *Scene of the Crime* (Evening Street Press), *Harbingers* (Blue Light Press), *Camille Abroad* (FutureCycle Press), *Like a B Movie* (FutureCycle Press). Forthcoming: *Camille Mobilizes* (Dec. 2018), (FutureCycle Press, 2018). jlagier.net

Mary Elizabeth Lang (53) earned her MFA in Poetry from Bennington Writing Seminars. Her poetry and memoirs have appeared in *Comstock Review, Ekphrasis, The Prose Poem, Connecticut Review, Naugatuck River Review, The Sun* and various anthologies. Books include *Under Red Cedars* (2008) and *Permanent Guests* (2018).

Gayle Lauradunn's (31) *Reaching for Air* was named a Finalist by the Texas Institute of Letters for Best First Book of Poetry. *All the Wild and Holy: A Life of Eunice Williams, 1696-1785* was awarded Honorable Mention for the May Sarton Poetry Prize. She was the co-organizer of the first National Women's Multicultural Poetry Festival, 1974. For her doctorate she created a high school curriculum using 20th century American poetry to teach about gender, class, and race.

Wayne Lee (10) (wayneleepoet.com) is a Canadian/American who lives in Hillsboro, Oregon. He has worked as a commercial fisherman, journalist, teacher, anodizing technician, public information officer, wedding officiant and tutoring company owner. Lee's poems have appeared in *Tupelo Press, The New Guard, Adobe Walls, Slipstream* and other journals and anthologies.

Elaine Leith (174) received her AA in English Literature from El Camino Community College in 1995 and went on to study English Literature, Anthropology and Linguistics at Cal State Dominguez Hills and due to illness and failing eyesight, I left college in 2000. Born in a small town in Oregon 67 years ago. I am visually impaired. I started writing poetry when I was 14. My stepmother, whom I knew as mom, became my greatest challenge. When she was stricken with dementia I found my anger towards her melt into forgiveness and even endearment.

Lennart Lundh (52, 58, 142) is a poet, short-fictionist, historian, and photographer. His work has appeared internationally since 1965.

Kathy Lundy Derengowski's (82, 182) work has appeared in *Summation,* the ekphrasis anthology of the Escondido Arts Partnership. *California Quarterly, Silver Birch Press, Turtle Light Press* and the *Journal of Modern Poetry.* She has won awards from the California State Poetry Society and been a finalist in the San Diego Book Awards poetry chapbook category.

Jennifer Maloney (178) lives and writes in Rochester, NY. Her work can be read in the Spring 2018 edition of *Aaduna.org*, edited by William Berry, Jr., volumes 4 and 5 of the Poets Speak...While We Still Can anthology series, edited by John Roche and Jules Nyquist, *A Flash of Dark, Volume 2*, edited by Scott W. Williams, and *ImageOutWrite, Volume 7*, edited by Jessica Heatly. She is happily serving as the current President of Just Poets, Inc., based in Rochester, and is thrilled to have found her voice again after many years of silence.

John Macker's (23) most recent publications are *Gorge Songs* (with Denver woodblock artist Leon Loughridge), *Disassembled Badlands* and *Blood in the Mix* (with Lawrence Welsh). Upcoming: *The Blues Drink Your Dreams Away* (Spartan Press, Kansas City). His essays on poets and poetics have appeared in *Miriam's Well, Cultural Weekly, Malpais Review* and *Lummox Journal*.

Catfish McDaris (40) won the Thelonius Monk Award in 2015. He's been active in the small press world for 25 years. He's recently been translated into Spanish, French, Polish, Swedish, Arabic, Bengali, Mandarin, Yoruba, Tagalog, Esperanto, and Italian. He's an editor at Ramingo's Porch and odditor at Odd Press.

Daniel McGinn (1, 65, 80) has a MFA in writing from Vermont College of Fine Arts. Both of his parents have been diagnosed with Alzheimer's disease; his Mother died from Alzheimer's in 2013. Daniel and his wife of 41 years, the poet and painter Lori McGinn, live with—and care for—his father.

Mary McGinnis, (43, 67, 143) the first recipient of the Gratitude Award from the NM Literary Arts Board in 2009, lives and writes in New Mexico. Besides appearing in over 70 magazines and anthologies, she has published three full-length collections: *Listening for Cactus, October Again, See with Your Whole Body, Breath of Willow*.

Caryl McHarney (49, 161) Drawings Period—shows at the Art Institute of Chicago, Museum of Modern Art, New York City.
Stoneware and Metals Period—many shows in New Mexico
Glass Period—St. Marks-on-the-Mesa windows, Albuquerque
Crane Period—Artist-in-Residence Rowe Audubon Sanctuary, Nebraska
Teaching Period - book design to create reading materials in Native Languages for thirty-two tribes in the United States and the Islands of the Pacific then called Micronesia.

Kelly Morgan (33) created this painting as a high school student, several years after her grandmother's death. In it, she explored what she imagined it must have felt like for her as her memories became disorganized and fragmented, and what it would be like to struggle to remember one's past.

Valarie Morris (186) writes prose poetry, librettos, music compositions, performance pieces, articles, short stories, interviews, and technical documents. Ballowe/Mitchell commissioned her science fantasy work, *The 8-Minute Genetically-Modified Opera*. Four important women in Jewish history sang their stories to music reflecting their eras in her *Voices of Shekhinah: Four Illuminations,* commissioned by the Tifereth Israel Community Orchestra and funded in part by an American Music Center grant. Her writings have appeared in a variety of publications, including *Sojourner, Strings, Mills Quarterly, New Mexico Free Press* and *'Round the Roundhouse.*

Carol Moscrip (192) came to San Diego six years ago and immediately found SDWI, Thursday Writers, and Dime Stories all thanks to friend and mentor Judy Reeves. Carol has published poems in *San Diego Poetry Annual* as well as in *A Year in Ink in 2018.* She is a recent Pushcart nominee.

Joseph Murray (56, 169) is a retired college professor who currently teaches and conducts meditation groups in Las Cruces, NM. His lyric and prose poems have appeared in *Common Ground, Branches,* and its *Best of Branches,* and *Nebo.* He is a member of Desert Writers, based in Las Cruces.

Bill Nevins, (37) born and raised in Stamford Connecticut, has been living in New Mexico since 1996. Bill has lived through the horrors of strict Roman Catholicism and of the Trump Administration as well as war and brief periods of peace. He remembers what merits remembrance, and "lets the rough side drag". His poems appear in many magazines, in his book *Heartbreak Ridge* (Swimming With Elephants Publications) and in his forthcoming 2019 book from Salmon Poetry of Ireland. He also was in the movie *Committing Poetry in Times of War.* He lives in Angel Fire and Albuquerque New Mexico. bill_nevins@yahoo.com

Suzanne Niedzielska, Ph.D., (136) sometime professor of philosophy, retired IT director for public and private enterprises, evolving early music instrumentalist, also works as a poet in English, chiefly in cross-cultural forms, such as the haiku from Japan, the Arabic, then Indian ghazal, and later European forms such as the sonnet.

Jim Nye (128) served in the 1st BN; 3rd INF. (Honor Guard) in Washington D.C.; 101st ABN, 2nd 502 and 5th Special Forces (MAC SOG) in Vietnam. He has written two books of poetry, *AFTERSHOCK* (Cinco Puntes Press) and *EATING THE ASHES* (Grandma Moses Press).He is married to Joan with a daughter, Jennifer, son-in-law, Adam, and two grandchildren, Lucy and Asher.

Jules Nyquist (13) is the founder of Jules' Poetry Playhouse, LLC, a place for poetry and play in Albuquerque, New Mexico. She took her MFA in Writing and Literature from Bennington College, Vermont. Her website is www.julesnyquist.com

Mary Oertel-Kirschner (42) is a poet, painter, and novelist. Her first mystery, *Never Too Old*, was published in 2017, and she is currently at work on a sequel. Her poems have appeared in several collections including *Quartet, Quintet, Fixed and Free, Santa Fe Literary Review, Sin Fronteras,* and *Adobe Walls*.

Marilyn C. O'Leary (164) has co-authored four books of poetry and two memoir/self-help books. She has published a poetry memoir about the passing of her husband titled *No One to Wake* and also has published an eBook of essays, *Love and Fun*. She is a professional life coach and lives in Albuquerque, NM.

Marmika Paskiewicz (30, 146, 181) writes in Santa Fe, NM. She watched her husband and partner of 30 years develop what used to be called early-onset Alzheimer's and followed his heart-breaking deterioration, always feeling he was still there, always fighting that reptile in his brain.

Andi Penner (50, 94) has been writing poetry for many years, long before moving to New Mexico which she now calls her "heart's home." Mercury Heartlink has published her books *When East Was North* (2012) and *Rabbit Sun Lotus Moon* (2017). The two poems included here honor her mother-in-law, and her father respectively.

In 1990 **Bernadette Perez** (120) received the Silver Poet Award from World of Poetry. Her work has appeared in *The Wishing Well; Musings in 2010,* Small Canyons Anthology in 2013, *Poems 4 Peace in 2014. Fixed and Free Anthology in 2015.* She is the President of the New Mexico State Poetry Society and member of Rio Grande Valencia Poets since 2005.

KAREN PETERSEN (81) has traveled the world extensively, publishing both nationally and internationally in a variety of publications. Most recently, her poems and short stories have been published in *The Manzano Mountain Review* in the USA, *The Bosphorus Review* in Istanbul, *Antiphon* in the UK, *The Wild Word* in Berlin, and *A New Ulster* in Northern Ireland. New work will be appearing later this year in the *Saranac Review* in the USA and *Idiom 23* in Australia. Her poems have been translated into Persian and Spanish. She holds a B.A. in Philosophy and Classics from Vassar College and an M.S. from Columbia University's Graduate School of Journalism.

Sylvia Ramos Cruz (100) writes poems inspired by art, nature, women's lives, and every-day injustices. Many reflect her life in Puerto Rico, New York and New Mexico. Her award winning work appears in local and national publications, including *Persimmon Tree, Malpais Review, Small Canyons Haiku Anthology, Encore: Prize Poems 2017, Poets Speak* anthologies, *and the Journal of Latina Critical Feminism*. Her ongoing project—writing haibun about her journeys to visit Historic NM Women road markers—combines her passions: poetry, feminism and driving the open road. She is a retired general surgeon, avid gardener, and women's rights activist.

Wendy Rainey's (74, 102) poetry has been published or is forthcoming in *Trailer Park Quarterly*, *Nerve Cowboy*, *Chiron Review*, and several other journals and anthologies. Her book, *Hollywood Church: Short Stories and Poems*, was published by Vainglory Press in 2015. She is a contributing poetry editor on *Chiron Review*.

Jim Ransom (77) was born in Las Vegas, New Mexico, educated at UNM and Yale, and taught for many years in the English department at Haverford College. His poems have appeared recently in *The Wallace Stevens Journal* and with the Telepoem Project. He lives in Santa Fe, New Mexico.

Janet Ruth (70, 130) is an emeritus research ornithologist, living in New Mexico. Her writing focuses on connections to the natural world. She has recent poems in *The Ekphrastic Review*, and in *Manzano Mountain Review*, *The Heron's Nest*, and regional publications including the *Poets Speak Anthology* and *Weaving the Terrain*. This summer she published her first book—*Feathered Dreams: Celebrating Birds in Poems, Stories & Images*.

Miriam Sagan (134, 152, 154) is the author of 30 published books, including the novel *Black Rainbow* (Sherman Asher, 2015) and *Geographic: A Memoir of Time and Space* (Casa de Snapdragon). which won the 2016 Arizona/New Mexico Book Award in Poetry. She founded and headed the creative writing program at Santa Fe Community College until her retirement in 2016 Her blog *Miriam's Well* (http://miriamswell.wordpress.com) has 1500 daily readers.

Georgia Santa-Maria (4, 32) is a Native New Mexican, and is an artist, photographer and writer. She has been published in many anthologies Her books include *Lichen Kisses 2013*, *Dowsing* (Lummox Press, 2017) and *Berlin Poems and Photographs*, co-written with Merimee Moffitt, She was the recipient of the Lummox Poetry Prize in 2016, and a First Place winner in 2018 with New Mexico Press Women for "Photography with Related Text," for *Berlin Poems and Photographs,* and an Honorable mention for the same from The National Federation of Press Women. She is now working on four other books.

Anne Shaughnessy's (44, 98, 170) writing has appeared in *The Arkansas Review*, *The Barefoot Review*, *Borderline Poetry Magazine*, and *Illya's Honey*. She won the Dallas Community Poets Award and held a residency at The Norman Mailer Center. She holds an MFA from Emerson College and a BA from Middlebury College.

Larry Schulte (41) is a visual artist, who began experimenting with words a few years ago. He studied with poet Hermine Meinhard in New York City for several years. Since moving to New Mexico in 2015, he has created poetry at the University of New Mexico with Michelle Brooks, Stephen Benz, Lisa Chavez and Diane Thiel.

Janet Simon (175) Began practicing podiatric medicine in Albuquerque, New Mexico in 1991 and has recently merged practice with the New Mexico Foot and Ankle Institute. Personal experience with caregiving of mom with dementia and many other patients.

Mary Strong Jackson's work has appeared in journals and anthologies in the United States and England. Her chapbooks include, *From Other Tongues, The Never-Ending Poem by the Poets of Everything, Witnesses, No Buried Dogs, Between Door and Frame,* and *Clippings.* More of her writing is available at strongjacksonpoet.wordpress.com. Mary lives near Santa Fe, New Mexico.

Richard Vargas (20) received his MFA from the University of New Mexico, 2010. He was recipient of the 2011 Taos Summer Writers' Conference's Hispanic Writer Award, was on the faculty of the 2012 10th National Latino Writers Conference and facilitated a workshop at the 2015 Taos Summer Writers' Conference.

Scott Wiggerman (2, 160) is the author of three books of poetry, *Leaf and Beak: Sonnets, Presence,* and *Vegetables and Other Relationships;* and the editor of several volumes, including *Wingbeats: Exercises & Practice in Poetry, Bearing the Mask,* and *Weaving the Terrain.* Recent poems have appeared in *Softblow, Ocotillo Review, The Ghazal Page,* and *Allegro Poetry Magazine.* He lives in Albuquerque, New Mexico.

Martin Willitts Jr (112) has 20 chapbooks including the winner of the *Turtle Island Quarterly Editor's Choice Award, The Wire Fence Holding Back the World* (Flowstone Press, 2017), plus eleven full-length collections including *The Uncertain Lover* (Dos Madres Press, 2018), and *Home Coming Celebration* (FutureCycle Press, 2019).

Holly Wilson (132) is a retired professor who lives in Albuquerque, New Mexico, where she owns a small farm. She started writing poetry as a teenager, and has been active in the Albuquerque poetry community for many years. She published her first book of poetry in May 2018, *Assorted Snapshots"* a collection of poetry she wrote in the 70's, 80's, and 90's.

Andrena Zawinski's (122) poetry has received accolades for lyricism, form, spirituality, social concern. It has recently appeared in *Aeolian Harp, The Aurorean, Common Ground Review, Dallas Review, Mantis, Raven Chronicles, Verse Daily,* and elsewhere. Her latest collection is *Landings.* She has two previous award winning books: *Something About* and *Traveling in Reflected Light.*

ABOUT THE PRESS:

Beatlick Press: Writers with something to say!
Our press exists to honor and maintain the literary philosophy and principles of Beatlick Joe Speer: Publish the deserving; support art, don't wait for art to support you.In 2011 our original publication, *Backpack Trekker: A 60s Flashback,* brought Joe's only book to fruition after twenty years of labor. Born and raised, died and buried in Albuquerque, New Mexico, Beatlick Joe dedicated his life to literature. Beginning in his 20s he wrote and published independently in order to support the written word of talented and often underserved writers and poets. His publications are archived in five American universities and other public libraries. His personal library is curated in special collections at his alma mater, New Mexico State University.

Pamela Adams Hirst, publisher

Made in the USA
San Bernardino, CA
11 February 2019